THE RETURN OF THE MAGI

PUBLISHED BY
THE LOST LIBRARY
GLASTONBURY, ENGLAND

First Published in English by
Philip Allan. in 1930
This edition 2016

This facsimile edition has been carefully scanned
and reprinted in the traditional manner by
THE LOST LIBRARY
5 High Street,
Glastonbury UK BA6 9DP

The LOST LIBRARY is a publishing house based in
Glastonbury, UK, dedicated to the reproduction
of important rare esoteric and scholarly texts for
the discerning reader.

Cataloguing Information
The Return of the Magi
Maurice Magre

ISBN 978 1 906 62140 7

Printed and bound in Great Britain by
Clays Ltd, St Ives plc

THE LOST
LIBRARY

THE
RETURN OF THE MAGI

TRANSLATED FROM THE FRENCH

OF

MAURICE MAGRE

BY

REGINALD MERTON

CONTENTS

INTRODUCTION

From the earliest times a message has passed from the East to the West, like the water of a bountiful river, to indicate the true path to perfection. At times, under the drought of evil or the violent fervour of ignorance, the river has dried up and the thirsty have not drunk of the liberating water. There have been centuries during which but a single drop has reached them, brought by a brave man in the vessel of his heart. There have been times also when the water flowed abundantly, but no one was able to see the deep bed in which it ran.

It has been my intention to write the history of the heroic messengers who brought the message at the peril of their lives, braving the hatred of the malicious and the anger of the deliberately blind, as well as a more formidable enemy, their own frailty.

This history is incomplete, because many persons invested with a high mission have been forgotten or disregarded in the annals of history, and also because there are others of whose existence the author is ignorant. It does not include the history of the highest messengers, the founders of religions. The lives and the teachings of these are well known, and another account would not give new light to anyone.

I have made it my task to write of masters who are less exalted but nearer to ourselves. The inmost essence of those who are too great eludes us. We are tempted to liken them to gods and think of them no more owing to the distance which separates them from us. Even if we had more detailed knowledge of the enigmatic Lao Tse, who among us would think of imitating his mode of life? What one remembers of him—and remembers with a certain satisfaction—is that he had a bad temper. Buddha's meditation under his fig tree seems to us to have been of superhuman duration. We should have liked him to return, or to repent what he had done, after he left his wife Yasodhara. We are almost drowned in the infinite indulgence of his smile. Jesus also is too perfect. Why did he not sometimes take up again the scourge with which he drove the money-changers from the temple?

One learns more from the frailties and defects of great men than from those of their qualities that are inaccessible for ordinary humanity. When I read of an Albigensian adept denouncing under torture all who had helped and hidden him in his flight, I am first of all indignant at his lack of courage; but then I begin to wonder how I should have behaved myself if I had had molten lead poured into my mouth and my legs slowly broken in a specially constructed machine. And I have all the more feeling for this adept who was overcome by physical pain, and with whom I have at least this frailty in common.

I was deeply touched by the love of Cagliostro for Lorenza, because it gave me the means of weighing the value of that which he sacrificed for her. He was aware of the power given to man by chastity, and I can well imagine the remorse and the great bitterness that he must have felt when she sold him to the Inquisition. Even the innumerable cigarettes that Madame Blavatsky so untiringly smoked are evidence to me that it is possible, without despairing of oneself, sometimes to gratify the physical body, which one is at the same time attempting to conquer.

It is more profitable to study the history of the imperfect masters than that of the masters who were so near the gods that they have been enveloped in the clouds of the empyrean. Such as they were, these imperfect masters, they constituted the imperfect chain, broken sometimes by their own hand, that connects the thought of the West with the eternal truth of Brahma, which is as old as the appearance of man on earth.

This truth is propagated by different means, according to the epoch and according to the people. It has become known to us through the teachings of the Cabala, through the Greek Mysteries and through the Neo-Platonic philosophy. The Albigenses of Languedoc possessed it in all its purity. The Rosicrucians caught a glimpse of it through the darkness of their Christianity. It is widely and freely current now, though I should not estimate at higher than fifteen the number of people in France who earnestly endeavour to receive it. But in its different aspects this truth has always been one. It is the light from a single diamond shining through the prism of apparently different formulæ.

What has seemed to me to be the most remarkable feature in the history of this transmission of truth is the following phenomenon, which is ceaselessly repeated.

Whenever the eternal wisdom of the East is presented to men—whether in the words of a prophet, or in the teachings of a sect, or in the form of a book—it arouses indignation. And the freer the truth from dross—the more beautiful, the more moral, in the noblest sense of that much profaned word—the higher the wave of indignation. Just as a worm gets into a ripe fruit and gnaws its heart, so an obscure agency slanders the prophet, breaks up the sect, parodies the thought contained in the book.

This phenomenon seems to be due to the working of a conscious will. In order to turn Christians from Apollonius of Tyana, the Fathers of the Church misrepresented all his actions and contrasted him with Jesus. Corruption crept into the Order of the Templars and served to justify, in external appearance, the charges brought by the King of France and the Pope. Jesuits penetrated among the Rosicrucians (where, thanks to their virtues of patience and humility, they attained prominent positions), transformed the symbolism of the Order, diverted it from its philosophic aim and turned it into a meaningless religious group. In modern theosophy an inner current has recently declared itself which tends to reduce theosophy to a kind of esoteric Catholicism. The only exception to this rule is seen in the case of the Albigenses, the hatred aroused by whom was so intense that they were exterminated to the last man, and even their descendants were exterminated. Everywhere the idea is transformed into narrow dogma, becomes petrified in dead ritual, materialised in ceremonial and genuflexions, in candles and incense. The letter stifles the spirit. So in the Middle Ages pure Christian ideas were stifled by the sacerdotal pomp of the Church.

But what is this will, which envelops movements

towards the human ideal and opposes them, either by force or by guile ?

Belief in these messengers involves belief in those who have sent them. Since the earliest ages of the history of humanity, in spite of wars and cataclysms, men more highly developed than ourselves have been the depositaries of the ancient wisdom which has been bequeathed to them down the centuries. Tradition relates that there exist seven brotherhoods of these wise men, the most important of which inhabits an unknown monastery in the Himalayas. These masters, who are more learned than we in the laws of Nature, more spiritualised, work at the development of other men to the extent permitted by their means, which are limited, and by our own capacity, which is extremely small. They are neither gods nor even demi-gods ; they are our fellows, but with more knowledge, more wisdom, more love. They desire us to partake of the fruit of truth, which is so difficult to cultivate and is so jealously preserved ; that is why they send into the world messengers entrusted with the task of spreading their teaching.

Human ignorance is so great that these messengers have always been received with contempt and derision. An arrogant love of unenlightenment is the characteristic of the Western races. But if the history of these messengers is followed, it will be seen that it is not only blind ignorance which has thwarted their efforts, but a hostile will, possessed of activity and intelligence. We are, therefore, justified in supposing that in opposition to the masters who turn men towards the spirit there are other masters, of another order, who have an opposite ideal, which, on our level of development, we may call evil. They represent the power of retrogression, which contests our spiritual progress. Whenever a man tries to free himself of matter and return to the divine unity —which is the goal of all religions and all occult systems— these masters hinder him and set up an ideal of individualism, a standard of excessive material enjoyment. To the ascetic in search of God they oppose the superman, the artist or the conqueror, who finds sublime pleasure in the egoistic aggrandisement of his being.

And it may be that these masters also send messengers. In which case the messengers would not only be representatives of egoism, eulogists of physical pleasure like some of the Roman poets, insane hedonists like Nero, philosophers like Nietzsche; they would be conscious destroyers of thought, men who may be observed throughout history impeding the activity of the mind. Among them would no doubt be the Chinese Emperor Che Hoang Ti, who, at the end of the third century before Christ, had a search made in his empire for the sacred books of China, of which he then proceeded to make an immense *auto da fe*. Among educated men his name endured as a symbol of horror. Another such was the Roman Emperor Diocletian, who destroyed the books dealing with the ancient occult science and condemned to death all found in possession of them. Such, too, was the canonised Bishop Cyril, who persecuted the philosophers of the Alexandrine school and destroyed the school, which represented the highest point of truth reached by man. Innocent III, Torquemada, the Emir Almohade Yacoub, who put philosophers to death, Hakem, Caliph of Egypt, that enemy of progress, whose greatest pleasure was to vilify and degrade, and a thousand others, may have been such messengers. Many of them exercised with love and faithfulness their innate hatred of the spirit. Sometimes they were kind-hearted people; when they had parents and children, they loved them; for the laws of instinct are common to all mankind, and true evil and true good operate on a quite different plane from that on which we usually place them.

Moreover, it may be that from a much higher point of view the white brotherhoods and the brotherhoods of evil, the initiates of God and the initiates of egoism, meet after their long separate journeys and realise that their paths are thenceforward one.

In the centuries to come the ascetic Albigensian will walk hand in hand with the proud bishop who had him burned at the stake. The idol Baphomet with his double face, symbol of the two currents that divide man, will be seen once more on the altar of the Templars. The Rosicrucian alchemist will no longer listen for the step of the Inquisitor in the street outside. There will be no more need of messengers to bring truth to the world because the purport of the message will be graven beforehand in the souls of men.

I apologise for the deep feeling with which I have written certain passages in this book, notably in the section which concerns the Albigenses. But I feel indignant at a great injustice which has never been remedied and seems unlikely to be remedied. Those self-controlled, unassuming men who lived in Southern France during the thirteenth century, whose practical rule was poverty and whose ideal was love of their fellow-men, were exterminated, and calumny has triumphantly wiped out even their name and their memory. Calumny has been so active and so skilful that the descendants of these wonderful men are unaware of the noble history of their ancestors; and when they wish to learn it it is presented in such a fashion that they blush at their extraordinary past. Through an analogous injustice the names of Apollonius of Tyana and of the Comte de Saint-Germain have been tarnished, or tainted with the suspicion of charlatanism.

May this book, imperfect as it is, light up the lives of those who died for a high ideal and who have not even had the posthumous reward of being useful to their unenlightened descendants! May it restore to the imperfect masters, whose lives I have traced in outline, a portion of the glory that is their due, which has been withheld from them because they were sometimes weak and passion-ridden, because they were human like us! May it show that in imperfection there may be greatness, that the face of the charlatan, if he is sincere, holds warmer comfort than the austerity of the scholar or the priest, and that the message of love and truth is an encouragement to us which is all the greater in that it is transmitted to man by a man!

APOLLONIUS OF TYANA

HIS YOUTH

THE voice which had one night cried to the ship's captain, "Pan, great Pan is dead!" still re-echoed over the Tyrrhenian sea; the three magi of Chaldæa had hardly climbed their towers after their journey to Bethlehem, when Apollonius was born in the little town of Tyana.

According to legend, great prodigies marked his birth. The most remarkable, because it is quite credible and therefore ceases to be a prodigy, seems to me worthy of being set down here. Just before he was born his mother was walking in a meadow; she lay down on the grass and went to sleep. Some wild swans, at the end of a long flight, approached her and by their cries and the beating of their wings awakened her so suddenly that the infant Apollonius was born before his time. Possibly —for there is a relation between the birth of certain persons and the life which surrounds them—these swans had foreseen and marked by their presence the fact that on that day was to be born a being whose soul would be as white as their own plumage and who, like them, would be a glorious wanderer.

Apollonius, exceptionally, received the gift of beauty. Men with the seal of the spirit are apt to be near-sighted, disproportioned, deformed. It is as though their inner fire causes irregularities in their physical bodies. And their career is accompanied by vague murmurings to the effect that they have followed the barren path of thought only because the path of pleasure was closed to them. But there was nothing of that sort said of this favoured among the children of Greece. And the renown of his beauty and intelligence grew so great that the words, "Whither do you hurry? Are you on your way to see the young man?" became proverbial in Cappadocia.

Another unusual gift was that of a great fortune. His father was one of the richest men in the province, so that his childhood was spent surrounded by luxury. He lacked nothing, neither learned masters to teach him nor the invaluable possibility of dreaming, which is given by leisure. Certain virtues devolve only on the few. In order to distribute his fortune among others a man must first have the good luck to possess a fortune. But every quality has its defect. From his early education Apollonius retained a leaning towards the aristocratic, a foible for greatness, which impelled him, on his travels, to hasten, before doing anything else, to visit the monarch of the country in which he happened to be, and, later at Rome, to become the counsellor of the Emperors.

When he was fourteen his father sent him to Tarsus to finish his education. Tarsus, as well as being a town of study was also a town of pleasure, and life there was soft and luxurious for a rich young man. On the banks of the Cydnus, in an avenue bordered with orange trees, students of philosophy discussed Pythagoras and Plato with young women in coloured tunics slashed to the hip, wearing Egyptian high triangular combs in their hair. The climate was hot, morals free, love easy. But the young Apollonius was not carried away by this. He showed at Tarsus a precocious puritanism from which he never deviated subsequently. In his opinion the wine flowed in too great abundance, wine that veils the clarity of thought and hinders the soaring of the spirit. Perhaps he was disturbed one evening by a face that was too beautiful and thought that if he once allowed himself to lie in a woman's lap and loosen the golden clasp of a silken tunic, he would be tempted to the end of his days to repeat the experience.

By his fourteenth year he was probably aware of the existence of the two different paths and weighed up all the riches of the mind, the time, the living energy, that are lost by love. He must have learned the inverse relation that exists between the gift of clairvoyance and love. And no doubt also he did not feel the need for enriching the mind through the heart. He resolved to remain chaste, and he seems to have kept his resolution.

Men of austere virtue—if, indeed, the absence of attraction by women can be called virtue—often find no difficulty in practising this virtue because they lack the fires which burn in other men. Of what possibilities of knowledge are those men deprived who at the outset of their lives adopt a rule of chastity ? Buddha married the beautiful Yasodhara and loved her tenderly. He even had other wives, in accordance with the custom of his country. Confucius was married to the obedient Ki Koo, and Socrates had two wives, in accordance with the laws of Athens, the charming Myrto and the bad-tempered Xanthippe. Plato made no profession of chastity, and Pythagoras did not include it among the essential rules of his school; for tradition relates that he was married to Theano and that he even laid down a series of precepts for conjugal life. So that it was his own prudence, his own extreme regard for spiritual safety, that impelled the young man of Tyana to keep his virginity, a condition which was exacted only from vestals and Pythian priestesses.

He took up his quarters at Ægæ with his Epicurean master Euxenes. Ægæ possessed a temple of Æsculapius, the priests of which were philosophers and doctors of the Pythagorean school. Men came from all Greece, Syria, and even Alexandria to consult them. There were pilgrimages, wholesale healings, an atmosphere of psychical phenomena and miracle. The priests of Ægæ healed by the laying on of hands and by the application of the power of thought, which was a science with them. They practised magic, studied the art of the interpretation of dreams, as well as the more subtle art of inducing them and extracting the prophetic element. They were the heirs of an ancient knowledge, of which the teaching was oral, which came from the old Orphic mysteries, and the secret of which had to be jealously guarded by the disciple who received it.*

The school of Pythagoras formed at that time a secret community with several stages of initiation, the members of which recognised one another by certain signs and used a symbolical language in order that the doctrine might remain unintelligible to the profane. Music, geometry and astronomy were the sciences recommended by the Pythagoreans as best adapted to prepare the soul for the reception of supra-sensory ideas. They taught detachment from material things, the doctrine of the

* The Pythagorean Timycha cut out her tongue rather than reveal to Dionysius the Elder the reason for the prohibition of beans in the rules of the community.

transmigration of souls through successive human bodies, the development of spiritual faculties through courage, temperance and fidelity to friendship. They discovered the relation of numbers to the phenomena of the universe, and they communicated with the souls of the dead and the spirits of Nature by means of ceremonies and incantations. The aim of their teachings was the enlargement and the purification of the inner man, his spiritual realisation.

Apollonius remained in the temple of Æsculapius, where he showed an astonishing gift for healing and clairvoyance and amazing eagerness to acquire the secret knowledge. He let his hair grow, abstained from the flesh of animals and from wine, and walked barefoot, clad only in linen clothes, giving up all that were made of wool. He even took a certain pride in having the outward appearance of a young prophet. However great a man may be, he does not disdain to dress his wisdom in the uniform of a wise man.

Euxenes tried in vain to deflect him into more moderate paths. In his opinion true wisdom was not so exacting a master. It might be reconciled with all the pleasures of life. Euxenes was one of those lean, insatiable hedonists, of whom the East produces so many, and for whom intellectual speculations were almost physical pleasures, of the same order as the choice of wine or women. He distrusted miracles, and what he most admired in Plato was the fact that the immortality of the soul had been discussed with the flowers and exquisite food of Agathon's banquet for setting.

Apollonius bore Euxenes no ill-will for being so unlike the perfect man who was his ideal. He bought him a villa surrounded by a garden outside Ægæ and gave him the money he required for his courtesans, his suppers and his poor friends.

He then imposed on himself the four years' silence which was necessary to obtain the final Pythagorean initiation. He became very celebrated. This celebrity grew uninterruptedly, a fact which he observed without displeasure. He made predictions that came true, quelled a rebellion by his mere presence, resuscitated a girl whose funeral passed him. But these were only recreations. Like all who passionately seek truth, he went back to its sources, insisted on knowing the origin of the divine waters of which he drank. Pythagoras travelled to Babylon and Egypt. But, according to a tradition preserved in all the temples, it was in India that he received the final word of wisdom ; it was from India that he brought the message that was to transform the men of Greece. Since then centuries had passed, bringing with them deep, regular waves of ignorance. The message has to be continually repeated. Apollonius felt that he was invested with the mission of setting off to seek the new words and bringing them back.

He had no doubt been very much affected by the stories with which the Greeks were then occupied concerning the Buddhist priest Zarmaros of Bargosa. Some years before the birth of Apollonius, Zarmaros had come to Athens with an Indian embassy bringing presents for the Emperor Augustus. He had been initiated into the Eleusinian mysteries, and then, as he was very old, he gave out that it was time for him to die, had a funeral pyre erected in a public square, and mounted it in the presence of the astonished Athenians.

The story of this death impelled Apollonius to see the country in which lived the wise men who had such a contempt for death. He made preparations to travel alone and on foot. The journey would be long and difficult, though less difficult than might be supposed. For in those days wise men and men of religion recognised a mutual kinship and formed secret communities in which the traveller found assistance and shelter from stage to stage.

Moreover, Apollonius knew where he was going. He took the route of Pythagoras, whose itinerary chance or the benevolence of a hidden power enabled him to discover.

Some distance from Antioch, while visiting, as his custom was, the ancient places that were sacred to the gods, he entered the half-abandoned temple of Daphnæan Apollo. He was charmed by the solitary beauty of the spot, the melancholy of the spring and the circle of very tall cypresses surrounding the temple. There was no one there but a half-peasant priest, who seemed somewhat crazy but in whom there still lived, like a forgotten lamp, the consciousness that he had to preserve a religious secret. When the priest returned from tilling his land he found Apollonius among his cypresses. He offered him hospitality for the night, which Apollonius accepted in order to be in the holy place next day before sunrise. For he thought that to commune with the gods, to receive their warnings and advice, the most propitious hour was that which precedes the birth of day. He was at prayer next day when the priest brought him the temple treasure, which had been preserved through tradition, handed down from father to son. This consisted of a few thin sheets of copper on which were cut figures and diagrams. The crazy priest had jealously preserved them till that moment, but in Apollonius he recognised the man worthy to receive the treasure which to him was incomprehensible.

By the light of the rising sun the Pythagorean deciphered on the copper sheets the record of his master's journey, an indication of the deserts and the high mountains to be crossed before he reached the river in which elephants disport themselves and on the banks of which grow apples as blue as the calyx of the hyacinth. He saw before him a description of the exact spot which he had to reach, of the monastery among the ten thousand monasteries in India which was the abode of the men who know.

Apollonius was to be the last Western emissary for centuries. After him the door was shut. Plotinus tried in vain two centuries later to follow in his steps behind the armies of the Emperor Gordianus, but was compelled to turn back. Thenceforward it was to be possible to create light only from the almost vanished fragments of the ancient wisdom. Darkness was about to fall for centuries on the Christian world.

APOLLONIUS IN THE "ABODE OF WISE MEN"

APOLLONIUS had just reached the little town of Mespila, which had once been Nineveh, "brilliant as the sun on a forest of palms," and was looking at the low houses built in past centuries by Salmanazar's slaves. The curve of a half-buried cupola emerged from the sand. Near by was the statue of an unknown goddess with two horns on her forehead, and among the broken mosaics a man was sitting. It was Damis,* who from that moment was to become his life's companion.

By virtue of some mysterious affinity a dog which you meet casually in the street turns, attaches itself obstinately to you and shows inexplicable faithfulness. Damis rose to his feet, saluted the man who was thenceforward to be his master, and was accepted by him as a guide to take him to Babylon.

He knew the way there perfectly, and he boasted, too, of knowing the languages spoken in the countries through which they would have to pass. Apollonius smiled and replied that he knew all the languages spoken by men and understood their silence as

* The life of Apollonius is known from the ingenuous stories of his disciple Damis. These stories were collected in the second century by Philostratus, who, at the request of the learned empress Julia Domna, wrote a life of Apollonius.

well. Damis was to realise a little later that Apollonius also possessed knowledge of the language of birds, and could read the great characters, dark against the blue of the sky, formed by the trajectory of their flight.

But the guide was to act as guide for the terrestrial journey only ; in their spiritual journey it was he who was to be guided. Damis was an ordinary man in quest of his fate, whatever that might be. If a troupe of travelling actors had happened to pass by he might have taken service with them as a dancer. But it was a wise man whom he met, and he dedicated himself to wisdom. Wisdom, however, never took much account of him. He did not penetrate below the surface of the mysteries with which he came into contact. Possibly because Apollonius always left him outside the door of the temples ; or else because his love of the marvellous prevented him understanding truth, which is more beautiful than fiction.

The two travellers saw the glistening silver-blue domes of Babylon ; they passed through its walls, spoke with the magi and set out on their journey again. They climbed mountains such as they had never seen before. The summits were veiled in clouds, but Apollonius remained unaffected by the gradual unfolding of their snowy immensities.

" When the soul is without blemish," he said, " it can rise far above the highest mountains."

They crossed the Indus and passed through countries whose coinage was of yellow and black copper and whose kings were clothed in white and despised ostentation. One evening, on a lonely river bank, they came on a brass stele inscribed with the words, " Here Alexander halted."

And when they had for many days followed the course of the Ganges, when they had climbed more hills and mountains, and met the single-horned wild ass, the fish with a blue crest like the peacock's, and the insect from whose body inflammable oil is made; when they had avoided the tiger with the precious stone in its skull —they saw in the middle of a plain a stone building with the same elevation as the Acropolis at Athens. They were, according to Philostratus' account, eighteen days' march from the Ganges.* A strange fog hovered above the place, and on the rocks surrounding it were the imprints of the faces, beards and bodies of men who appeared to have fallen. From a well with a bottom of red arsenic the sun drew a rainbow.

Apollonius and his companion had the feeling that the path by which they had come had disappeared behind them. They were in a place that was preserved by illusion, in which the countryside shifted its position and moved in order that the traveller might not be able to fix a landmark in it. Apollonius had at last reached the country of the wise men of India, of whom he was later to say:

" I have seen men who inhabit the earth, yet do not live on it, who are protected on all sides though they have no means of defence, and who nevertheless possess only what all men possess."

Then a young Indian advanced towards them; on his

* It may be noted that Tzigadzi, the great centre of Thibetan lamaseries, is about 18 days' march from the Ganges.

hand was a ring of gilded bamboo in the form of an anchor. He greeted Apollonius in Greek (for the men whose messenger he was had heard of his arrival) and conducted them to the community of wise men and to their head, Iarchas.

For several months Apollonius lived with the men who knew. It was here that he learned the science of the spirit, the capacities hidden in the heart of man and the means of developing them, in order to live as the gods live. It was from Iarchas that he received the mission that was to send him wandering all his life long among the temples of the Mediterranean countries, for the purpose of dematerialising religion, restoring its former purity. It was here that he learned to pronounce the ineffable name, the secret of which confers on its possessor supreme power over men and the capacity of dominion over invisible beings.

When he left his Indian hosts, Apollonius had the certain knowledge that he would be able to remain in communication with them.

" I came to you by land," he said; " and you have opened to me not only the way of the sea but, through your wisdom, the way to heaven. All these things I will bring back to the Greeks, and if I have not drunk in vain of the cup of Tantalus I shall continue to speak with you as though you were present."

The wise men, on the threshold of their valley of meditation, gave them white camels on which to cross India.

They returned by the Red Sea, in which the Great Bear is not reflected and where at mid-day men cast no shadow on the deck of their ship. They saw the country of the Orites, where the rivers abound with copper; Stobera, the city of the Ichthyophagi; and the port of Balara, surrounded with myrtle and laurel, where are found shell fish with white shells and a pearl in the place of the heart.

HIS MISSION

APOLLONIUS returned from India charged with a task of the magical order, which, within the knowledge of man, he was to be the only person to accomplish. It is possible that Pythagoras before him had been invested with the same mission, which he discharged during his travels. But that we shall never know.

Iarchas had shown him in a cell of his monastery a young shining-eyed ascetic whose intellectual faculties were more extraordinary than those of any of the other wise men in the community, but who nevertheless was unable to attain a state of serene meditation. Sometimes he even cursed his intelligence and declared it useless. He suffered from perpetual restlessness, which could not be allayed. Apollonius had enquired the identity of this ascetic and the reason for his sufferings.

"He suffers from an injustice done him in a previous life," was Iarchas' answer. "He was Palamedes, the greatest and the wisest of the Greeks. His name is forgotten now and his tomb abandoned, and Homer makes no mention of him in his history of the Trojan War."

This was an example of the danger of knowledge. Apollonius might have replied:

"How grateful should we be to Nature, who has drawn over man the veil of oblivion simultaneously with the veil of death and has so preserved him from the evil consequences of the life he leaves behind him! How worthy of compassion is he who is developed sufficiently to read the past, but insufficiently to judge an old injustice with indifference."

Apollonius undertook to repair the injustice done to Palamedes, though he only acted according to the instructions he had received. He had learned from Iarchas the art of imprisoning in objects spiritual influences which had the power to act at a distance and across time. In certain places, preferably sanctuaries which already contained magnetic influences of religious origin, he was to lay talismans intended to perpetuate the active force which had been enclosed in them. Similarly, in ancient tombs or sacred chambers he would find talismans which had been laid there by former messengers of the spirit.

The tombs of heroes long retain in their stones, in the leaves of surrounding trees, in their solitary atmosphere, the ideal of the man who has become dust. That is the reason why pilgrims who cross the earth in fulfilment of a vow and prostrate themselves before the monument of some revered person, always bring back in their empty hands immaterial riches which they alone can see.

A little later Christianity was to revive these practices of ancient magic and extend their use enormously with the worship of the saints and the adoration of relics. But it never found out the secret of Apollonius.

His first thought after reaching Smyrna was to go to Troy. His travels in India had increased his fame, and many disciples accompanied him. They embarked with him on a ship which carried them to the coast of Æolia, opposite Lesbos, not far from the little port of Methymna. They arrived at sunset in a deserted bay, and Apollonius requested to be left alone on shore in order that he might meditate in the hour before dawn, when the thoughts of the spirits of the dead and of higher powers reach men pure enough to receive them.

It was in this place that Palamedes lay buried; Palamedes, of whose very name Homer was unaware; the poet and the scholar, who had been the victim of Ulysses, the man of action. The man who had invented different methods of calculation, fire-signals and the game of chess, the most inventive of all the Greeks, had been stoned before the walls of Troy through a false accusation of treason brought by Ulysses.* That creative intelligence should have gone unappreciated; that the winged gifts of this inventor of science and beauty should have been stifled by jealousy, and no reparation made after his death—was a racial crime which it was necessary to set right, a blot on the history of mankind which would become greater as men's culture progressed, and which it was the duty of a wise man's hand to wipe out.

At dawn Apollonius indicated the spot near the sea where they were to dig, and a statue of Palamedes, a cubit high, was found. It was set up in its former position, in which Philostratus, two centuries later, bears witness that he saw it. The statue of the unappreciated hero standing opposite the sea was for long a proof to travellers interested in the memorials of primitive Greece that sooner or later justice is done to those who have lit the first lamps of enlightenment. And perhaps in a cell in the abode of wise men a taciturn ascetic felt an unfamiliar consolation fall on him like a ray of the Æolian sun.

* Palamedes detected Ulysses' feigned madness. Ulysses out of revenge forged a letter from Priam, King of Troy, and hid it in Palamedes' tent. Whereupon Palamedes was stoned to death.—*Trans.*

Where did Apollonius, during his travels throughout the world, lay the talismans whose radiations were to ensure man's spirituality? Is it to him that the impression is to be ascribed that one feels at Pæstum (where he stayed), before the now deserted Temple of Neptune? The man who breathes in its silence, touches its Pentelican marble, even now finds himself compelled to look within himself, where, in the depths of his heart, he catches a glimpse of another deserted temple, set before a sea that is not so definite as the Mediterranean. It is the same with the Lérin Islands, where Apollonius stayed because he thought (though without grounds) that that favoured spot off the Gallic coast was to become a centre of future civilisation. Here, soon after his visit, was founded the monastery of Saint-Honorat, which has endured through the centuries.

The murmur of the cypresses in the avenue there is different from elsewhere, the colour of the stones is different; and if you lean over the well you feel the vibration of the eternal verities of life. Is this the result of the magic of Apollonius? It would, of course, be childish to assert that it is. All that can be said is that he applied, or tried to apply, a method the transcendence of which eludes us.

The ostensible and most easily intelligible aim that he pursued was that of unifying creeds, explaining symbols, showing the spirit behind the images of the gods of paganism, suppressing sacrifice and external forms, in order that all worship might participate in the Platonic union with divinity. For this purpose he went to all the holy places, in Syria, Egypt, Spain; he even reached the rock of Gades, which later was to become Cadiz, and was, according to Pliny, the last part of the continent that escaped the catastrophe of Atlantis.

Everywhere he received as he passed almost divine honours. His capacity for clairvoyance enabled him to make predictions which were verified by events and which had the effect of increasing his fame. He had no difficulty in escaping Nero's persecution of philosophers, and his admirers said that when confronted with the tribunal that was to try him, he was able, through his magic art, to erase the writing on the document on which his inditement was written. He acted as counsellor to Vespasian. He recognised the real nature of a vampire woman, who, in the form of a beautiful girl, incited his disciple Menippus to pleasure in order to drink his blood. He recognised also the personality of a recently dead and much-mourned king in a tame lion which was herbivorous, and very gentle and affectionate. He restored the true idea of love to a rich madman who wished solemnly to marry a statue. He exorcised a lecherous demon who instigated an inhabitant of Corcyra to attack all women he met. He healed a man who had just been bitten by a mad dog—which was an ordinary miracle. But he pursued the mad dog a long way in order to heal it, too, by plunging it into a river—which was a sign of exceptional kindness of heart. Imprisoned by Domitian and acquitted by the court which tried him, he disappeared immediately after being set free, either by using a trick of collective suggestion, like some fakirs, or else, wishing for rest after the emotions of his trial, by merely mingling unnoticed with the crowd.

At last, after a thousand natural miracles, easily accomplished, when he was more than eighty years old he accomplished the miracle of dying. It was a great miracle, for everyone believed him immortal. But perhaps after all this miracle was not accomplished, for at the end of his life Apollonius, like all the great adepts, disappeared without leaving a trace. The phenomenon of disappearance seems to have been particularly pleasing to him, and he did not fail to contrive it at the moment of death, the longest disappearance of all.

Some say that one evening he left his house in Ephesus, where he lived with two servants, and never entered it again. Others assert that the disappearance of his physical body took place in a temple of Dictynna, where he was spending a night in meditation.

No one has ever heard of the tomb of Apollonius, just as no one knows where Pythagoras died. Several Roman Emperors who admired Apollonius, notably Caracalla, who put up a temple to him, investigated the matter in vain.

It may be noted, though importance is not to be attached to the fact, that eleven centuries later there lived in Spain an Arab philosopher named Artephius, who claimed to be Apollonius of Tyana. This Artephius lived in Granada and Cadiz, where Apollonius had stayed for a long time. He stood in very high reputation among the hermetic philosophers of his day, who came from the most distant countries in order to consult him. Like Apollonius he professed the Pythagorean philosophy and studied the art of compounding talismans and divination by the characters of the planets and the song of birds. He had been able, he said, to prolong his life in a miraculous way by means of his knowledge of the philosopher's stone.

HIS WEAKNESS AND GREATNESS

"APOLLONIUS," Domitian asked when he appeared before him, "why do you not wear the same clothes as other people, but dress in special clothes of a singular kind?"

To the end of his days Apollonius felt the need of singling himself out from others, of attracting curiosity to his person. The higher men rise, the greater grows their pride and the more childish it remains.

As he entered Mesopotamia, the toll-collector on the bridge over the Euphrates asked him what he brought with him.

"Continence, justice, courage and patience," was the reply.

The collector, thinking of nothing but his tolls, said:

"Give me a list of these slaves."

Apollonius answered:

"They are not slaves; they are masters."

When he reached Babylon a high official of the king, whom he was about to visit, as his custom was, asked him what presents he brought. Apollonius replied:

"All the virtues."

"And do you suppose," said the official, "that he does not already possess them?"

"If he possesses them I will teach him how to use them."

He had two slaves, of whom he emancipated only one—a sign of semi-generosity.

Once, when in a garden in Ephesus, he saw by clairvoyance the murder of Domitian in Rome. "Strike the tyrant, strike him!" he cried joyfully, as though to encourage the distant murderer. Which shows that he did not profess the forgiveness of all offences.

His miracles were so numerous that some of them must have been done for the purpose of dazzling his followers, of adding to his fame. For his own personal advantage he made use of his knowledge of natural laws that were still unknown to his contemporaries. So, on the penultimate rung of the ladder of development, does self-love drag a man down again to the bottom.

Woe to those who, claiming disinterestedness, do not achieve total disinterestedness! Once on the path that leads to the heights, a man no longer has the right to look back; and a single selfish thought destroys the fruit of a whole life devoted to the love of mankind.

The world, for the spiritual development of which he worked so enthusiastically, has not done Apollonius full justice, and has even discussed sharply the perfect purity of his life. He was surrounded with hatred as well as with admiration. He made too many prophecies, even though they were precisely realised, performed too many marvellous tricks. The mediocre minds which create the reputations of great men insist that virtue shall be muffled in tedium and that it shall not be illumined by anything of the marvellous. If a man lacks the audacity or has too much sincerity to present himself as a god, he must be content to remain within the limits of honest humanity. If the philosophers glorified Apollonius, the

Christian world contrasted him with Jesus; while the ecclesiastical historians for centuries, even down to our own times, have made his name a synonym for charlatan and trickster, with a tenacity which should suffice to prove his greatness of soul.

Renan, the last of these ecclesiastical historians, after calling him "a sort of Christ of paganism," retracts his words and says:

"If Apollonius had been sincere, we should know him through Pliny, Suetonius or Aulus Gellius, as we know Euphrates, Musonius and other philosophers."

But Renan forgets that neither Pliny nor Suetonius nor Aulus Gellius speaks of Jesus, whom, for all that, he regards as a sincere man. For my part, I think that man was "sincere" who never entered a temple without saying this prayer: "Grant, O gods, that I may have little and feel the need of nothing." For contempt of riches is a wonderful touchstone of man's virtue.

He was a sincere man who taught the immortality of the soul, but taught it with caution (in which he resembled Buddha), saying that it was useless to discuss too far this question and that of man's destiny after death, because he considered that that part of the truth which was known to him was too deceptive.

He was a sincere man who said: "When the body is exhausted, the soul soars in ethereal space, full of contempt for the harsh, unhappy slavery it has suffered. But what are these things to you? You will know them when you are no more."

For him wisdom was "a sort of permanent state of inspiration," to attain which he prescribed chastity, a food of herbs and fruit, clothes as immaculate as the body and the soul.

He was a sincere man who laboured to separate the spiritual essence of his being and unite it with the divine spirit; who, ascribing an important part to the imagination, using it as a path to self-development, discerned in the smile on the face of a statue the spirit that lies behind form; who regarded material things, the contour of a landscape, the colour of rivers and of stars, the multiform earth, as the symbols of another, a purer world, of which they were but the reflections.

THE DAIMON

ALMOST all of us at least once in our lives, during a sleepless night or an illness, have heard a voice which, coming from nowhere, and, as it were, speaking silently, gives us advice, usually wise advice. It is always when we are in solitude and most often at moments of exaltation that this silent voice speaks. Certain men of genius have heard this voice near them so plainly and so often as to make them believe that an intelligent being was about them, directing them with inspired advice.

The Greeks called this being by the name of *daimon*, and the best-known of all, that which has been discussed at greatest length by the philosophers, was the *daimon* of Socrates.

" The favour of the gods," said Socrates, " has given me a marvellous gift, which has never left me since my childhood. It is a voice which, when it makes itself heard, deters me from what I am about to do and never urges me on."

He spoke familiarly of this *daimon*, joked about it and obeyed blindly the indications it gave. Eventually, his friends never took an important step without consulting it. But the *daimon* had its sympathies, and when it was unfavourable to the questioner it remained absolutely silent ; in that event it was quite impossible for Socrates to make it speak.

Of what order was this *daimon*, which manifested itself to Socrates in childhood but was heard by Apollonius of Tyana only after he had begun to put into practice the Pythagorean rules of life ?

" They are intermediate powers of a divine order. They fashion dreams, inspire soothsayers," says Apuleius.

" They are inferior immortals, called gods of the second rank, placed between earth and heaven," says Maximus of Tyre.

Plato thinks that a kind of spirit, which is separate from us, receives man at his birth, and follows him in life and after death. He calls it " the *daimon* which has received us as its portionment." It seems, therefore, to be analogous to the guardian angel of Christians.

Possibly the *daimon* is nothing but the higher part of man's spirit, that which is separated from the human element and is capable, through ecstasy, of becoming one with the universal spirit. To an organism that has been purified, therefore, it would be able in certain conditions to transmit both the vision of past events, the image of which happens to be accessible to it, and that portion of the future the causes of which are already in existence, and the effects of which are consequently foreseeable.

But the fact that the *daimon* had preferences among Socrates' friends, that it chose between them, seems to show that its intelligence was different from that of Socrates himself. Socrates often said that this inner voice, which many times deterred him from doing one thing, never incited him to do something else. Now it is a rule among adepts never to give any but negative advice ; for he who advises someone to do a thing not only takes upon himself the burden of the consequences, but deprives the man he advises of all merit in the action.

Apollonius believed that between the imperfection of man and the most exalted among the hierarchy of creation there existed intermediaries. One of his intermediaries was the ideal of beauty that we make for ourselves, an ideal which is formless, but is none the less real on another plane of life. This ideal was the *daimon*, the reality of which became the greater in proportion as the idea of it became the more powerful in its creator's mind.

Thus a sculptor with intuition who had a knowledge of magic might, in certain conditions, be able to give form to a creature of ideal beauty begotten by his own ideal.

In order then to steep oneself in the perfection of this creature there would be two methods: either to actualise it on the terrestrial plane by giving it a form; or to enter its ethereal domain by divesting oneself of form through the transformation of ecstasy.

Plotinus, Iamblichus, Prœlus and all the mystics of the Neo-Platonic school used the second method. They sought the beauty of the soul, strove to find the radiant inner ego, and thanks to the impetus of ecstasy they sometimes attained their aim.

It may be that certain workers of miracles who possessed an amazing secret used the first method and lived with a divine companion whom they had themselves made visible to their own human eyes. But they kept their secret to themselves. Those of them who spoke of it were regarded as mad and were imprisoned or burned. There were others, too, whose soul was impure and who created caricatures of the ideal and were haunted by monsters resembling them. The Middle Ages, when methods of ancient magic were still being handed down, are full of stories of men possessed, tormented by their own demons, which, once they were created, never died and attached themselves to their creator.

We shall never know to what order the *daimon* of Apollonius belonged; whether the being who advised him took on a form as chaste as himself and as beautiful as the statues of the gods which he liked to contemplate; or whether the voice came from a distant master who wished to see his pupil carry out the mission with which he had entrusted him.

"I shall continue to speak with you as though you were present," Apollonius had said as he left his Indian masters.

Was it their words that he heard at a distance? Did he by divine inspiration receive the influx of their wise thoughts? The man to whom he gave the name of Iarchas must often have brought the consolation of distant support to the untiring traveller, the wandering mystic. Even in Domitian's darkest cell there was a moment when a certain fluidity in the atmosphere indicated the light of dawn. The world was more silent, the walls became thinner, and the voice was heard:

"The greatest are those who never find their place, in times which are unpropitious to them. Nothing of the good that a man has done, and, more particularly, nothing of the good that he has thought, is lost, even if he is imprisoned or crucified for that good. But be not as the Hindu ascetic, who was unable to forget injustice. Because the word of the master Jesus will burn like a living flame deep into the hearts of Western humanity, you will be calumniated and forgotten. You will be contrasted with Him, and for centuries pious men will speak of you as a juggler or mountebank. But if you rise to the region where neither justice nor injustice exists, you will know that this is a matter of small importance. . . . It will be necessary for you to share also His sorrow, which is very great. He has been a thousand times more misunderstood than you, a thousand times worse betrayed. Make ready to approach Him on the day that is appointed in the Book without characters. Perhaps He will elect to speak with kings, and send you to teach poor fishermen. Then perhaps you will be crowned with the glory that you so ardently desired."

THE UNKNOWN MASTER OF THE ALBIGENSES

THE UNKNOWN MASTER OF THE ALBIGENSES

WAS there an unknown master whose words gave birth to the Catharist* truth? Did a master bring the eternal verities from the East to the inhabitants of Albi and Toulouse? Was he the man whom a peasant of Rouergue met by the roadside one evening as he was returning to his farm, the man who, according to the peasant's story to the Inquisition tribunal, had a strange persuasive power, the features of a Moor, and a bluish light around his head? Was he Pierre, the pupil of Abelard, who began teaching in the twelfth century? Was he one of those anonymous preachers who stopped at street corners in small towns to teach simple men that the poverty which brought them apparent unhappiness was the pledge of boundless bliss after death?

Was the true initiate, the great propagator of Catharism, Nicetas, the Bulgarian mystic who several times travelled through Southern France, laid the foundations of a new church at Saint-Felix de Caraman, and entrusted to certain men, whom he recognised as

* The origin of the word *Catharist* is obscure. Derived from the Greek *καθαρός*, clean, pure, it must have signified those who strive towards perfection, and been the name which the members of the sect originally gave themselves. Pronounced *Cazarist*, it may have been applied to the inhabitants of Cazères, a small town near Toulouse which was a centre of the heresy, and the use of the word was then extended, like the word *Albigenses*, to include all the heretics of Southern France.

being pure of heart, the book in which the spiritual doctrine was embodied? Nothing is known of him, except the deep impression left by his visit and the extension of the Catharist movement which followed his departure for Sicily.*

The greatest masters remain hidden, and in the origin of the Albigenses no one sublime personage can be found playing the rôle of initiator. Possibly, in virtue of the expansive force of truth, the heretical doctrines that came from the East crossed Europe, to invade France and spread to Germany, like wind-carried pollen which germinates wherever the ground is propitious.

In Greece the monk Niphon, a man full of wisdom and virtue, was condemned by the Patriarch Oxites to lose his beard, a mild and somewhat peculiar punishment. He was also imprisoned. But he was set free by another patriarch. His beard grew again, and his fiery preaching raised up disciples who travelled all over the world to spread his words.

Near Turin a fervent believer, a countess, who owned the castle of Monteforte, formed, with the help of a mystic named Girard, a community which attempted to lead the perfect life. In it all men were equal, and the goods of one belonged to the others. No meat was eaten, for they believed it wrong to take the lives of animals. No wine was drunk, for its fumes obscured the presence of the spirit. Life to them was a kind of penitence, and if a man did not desire eternally to enter new bodies, to

* It may be noted that it was after the visit of Nicetas to Sicily that the group of the *Faithful in love* was formed, whose doctrine had so much in common with Catharism. It is said that Frederick II, the protector of heretics, was an initiate. One of the masters of this group was Guido Cavalcanti, the friend and initiator of Dante.

reincarnate endlessly, it was necessary for him to attain to detachment from everything, for that alone would allow him to become united with God. It was necessary also, but only when a man had reached a certain degree of perfection, to abstain from marriage and from the act by which life is perpetuated.

The Archbishop of Milan conducted an expedition against the castle of Monteforte. He took the heretics prisoner and had them all burned at the stake. The chronicler of these facts remarks that the archbishop would have preferred to spare their lives, but does not explain why he did not do so.

It was then that the words of Girard, spoken before his death, were verified.

"It is not I alone whom the Holy Spirit visits. I have a large family on earth, and it comprises a great number of men to whom, on certain days and at certain times, the Spirit gives light."

This light became manifest throughout France.

An unknown woman came to Orleans, and after listening to her all the canons of the collegiate church of Sainte-Croix turned heretic. Two clerks named Etienne and Lisoi became the theologians of a new church which taught that Jehovah, the God of the Old Testament, was an evil God Who, after being unwise enough to create, concerned Himself solely with punishment; a church which rejected baptism and gave remission of sins only on condition of perfection of life.

At the order of King Robert these heretics were seized at a house in Orleans in which they were meeting. They were dragged off to a church, where Guarin, Bishop of Beauvais, interrogated them while their stake was being erected outside the town. Queen Constance waited before the church door for the condemned men to come out and with the end of her stick put out one of Etienne's eyes, for he had previously been her confessor and had caused her to run the risk of hearing false doctrine. The historian records that a nun preferred to renounce her heresy rather than be burned at the stake, but omits to tell us how many preferred death to renunciation.

The spirit breathed at random, touching the foolish as well as the wise. One day while the Breton Eon de Loudéac was attending mass in a church he fell asleep. The officiating priest had a loud, echoing voice, and Eon was awoken by it as it was pronouncing this sentence in the liturgy, "*Per eum qui venturus est judicare vivos et mortuos*" (through Him who is about to come to judge the living and the dead). In the word *eum* Eon fancied he heard his own name uttered. It was God bidding him judge the living and the dead, distinguish the pure from the impure. He rushed out of the church. His mission had begun.

He started preaching. He branded the wealth of the prelates, the harshness of the powerful. All who possessed property were no better than dead. He, Eon, conferred life by the laying on of hands. He judged, as God had directly bidden him. He expounded the Catharist doctrines, which had mysteriously come to him, and his sincerity, coupled with a kind of light-hearted wildness, made him popular wherever he went. Disciples gathered round him, and their number continually increased. After travelling through Brittany, Eon turned southwards. He camped with his disciples on moors and in forests. He organised a church of priests according to God, who possessed nothing and went almost naked, followed by a great crowd of the faithful.

The Archbishop of Rheims succeeded in dispersing the menace of these pure-living men. Pope Eugene III travelled to preside in person over the council which tried Eon. But to all questioning Eon merely replied that on him lay the duty, following upon the direct order of God, to judge the living and the dead.

In Flanders a certain Tanquelin, like Jesus, spoke with fishermen. He roused the people of the North to enthusiasm by proclaiming that the sacraments were useless and that women ought to be communised on account of the vanity of the pleasure obtained through them. But success turned his head. He returned to the taste for riches which he had begun by proscribing. This former apostle of simplicity assumed princely clothes, encircled his hair with a golden fillet and, one day, betrothed himself to the Virgin Mary before an image.

But it was in the region of Albi, Carcassonne and Toulouse that the mystic revolution took place. In the Périgord district there was Pons, at Toulouse Henri, at Castres Guillabert. But these men were scholars and philosophers, who expounded the wisdom of Catharism in writing. The Roman Church had shut its iron gates and raised the walls of its ever immutable principles. With the Catharist philosophy many intelligent people welcomed the possibility of disclosing by free research the spiritual meaning of the scriptures, and of solving the metaphysical problems which have haunted thinking men from the earliest times. Others, men who did not read books but observed and were shocked by the ostentation and immorality of the bishops, listened to the ascetics of the street corners because their souls were like the souls of the early Christians and because there was to be found in their words the pure doctrine of the master Jesus.

That which the Church called "the abominable epidemic leprosy of the south" manifested itself as an epidemic of unselfishness, a handing on of goodness, a chain of sacrifice.

A rich citizen of Carcassonne awoke in the night because he could no longer bear the thought of his riches when so many poor men had nothing. An inner voice told him that he must not lose a moment, an order which he obeyed scrupulously. He took up valuable pieces of furniture and carried them into the street, for anyone to take what he wished. As the night was dark he lit two lamps before his door in order to facilitate the wayfarer's choice; and as the street was deserted he fetched a trumpet and blew it in order that men might know that his property no longer belonged to him, that they might hasten to take it from him, and that the rising sun might shine on his redeeming poverty.

At Lavaur a half-dumb man succeeded in speaking and became eloquent in the desire to teach his fellow-men that not only is there a single life of suffering, but a man must reincarnate endlessly in different bodies if he does not escape from the inexorable wheel by attaining perfection in one life-time.

At Montauban a man named Querigut scandalised the town by handing over his wife, to whom he was devoted, to another man who loved her. He retired to a hill which was the haunt of wolves, where he ate berries and roots, and slept joyfully on the bare earth ; for, he said, a man learns from the companionship of wolves that the more the body suffers the higher the soul rises, and the more he subdues human love the more he gains divine love.

Buddhist renunciation became a moral law which spread with astonishing rapidity. From Bordeaux to the borders of Provence, in stern Languedoc, under the chestnuts of the Albi district and on the moors of Lauragais, the roads were full of ascetics walking barefoot, eager to tell their brothers what the spirit had revealed to them. And it was always the humble who received inspiration. The spirit was repelled by the magnetism which the gold of the Church released. On the other hand, it entered freely into the solitary mountain hut, into the artisan's little house backing on to the ramparts of a town, or into the peaceful monastery on the banks of the Ariège or the Garonne. In the poplar avenue and the stone cloister where walked a hundred shaven-headed monks, it breathed sometimes with such contagious power that it caused the gates to be shut and the garden and the chapel to be abandoned ; it transformed copyists of manuscripts and illuminators of missals into wandering prophets of the new heresy.

At the end of the twelfth century the words of the Pelagians, " Christ had nothing more than I have ; I can make myself divine by virtue," seemed essential to most men in Southern France. Estranged more and more from the God of the churches, the God to Whom were raised images that were too richly gilt in shrines that were too magnificent, the God of rich prelates and pitiless barons, they worshipped the inner God, Whose light grew brighter the more they lived pure lives filled with love for their fellow-men.

In the eyes of selfish men there can be no greater crime than a crime of disinterestedness and love. The hatred aroused by moral superiority shows no pity. The Christian Church with its priestly hierarchy, its richly endowed brotherhoods of monks, its powerful abbeys, could never forgive the Catharists for setting an example of asceticism that was greater than their own. There is no more cruel tragedy in history than that of the all but total annihilation of the Catharists by the King of France, the Pope, and the barons of the north.*

* Every history of France is a history of the unity of France, and not the impartial history of any particular district. The conception of unity causes the historian to violate the most elementary justice. The war with the Albigenses seems to have assisted the future unity of France. In those who write of it the indignation it arouses is by no means wholehearted. It is in every case summed up cursorily. There is a general wish to forget it. It is embarrassing. Even in the case of Michelet, the apostle of justice, there breaks through the contempt which northerners have always felt and still feel for the " eaters of garlic, oil and figs."

THE CRUSADE

AT that time the country which extended from the sea of Provence and the towers of Fréjus to the sea pines of Guyenne was, after the enlightened Spain of the Moors, the most civilised in the world. It was still illumined by the never-dying light of Athens and of Alexandria. The baths and triumphal arches of the Emperors had not fallen into ruin in its cities, and there was not a hill without a Roman statue among the vines and olives. Aristotle and Plato, who had been translated into Latin at Granada, were the food of its scholars. The towns had a municipal freedom that was unknown to the northern towns. At Toulouse the power of the *Capitouls* acted as a check to that of the Counts. The voluminous literature of the troubadours flourished even in the remotest villages of the Pyrenees. And the Saracen invaders had left behind them when they went the theorbo* of Damascus, on which the music of the Orient was played.

But to the men of the north, southerners seemed what they seem to-day: a garrulous, vain, idle race. Their gay lightheartedness seemed a want of seriousness, and their mysticism could be nothing but heretical. Among them survivals of paganism were more alive than elsewhere. Freedom of thought was greater; it manifested

* The theorbo was a two-necked musical instrument of the lute class.—*Trans.*

itself in the satirical lines of the poets, in the sermons of predicant monks, in popular movements that were so audacious, so lacking in respect, that it was possible for St. Bernard, after a triumphal journey through France, to be hooted by a crowd in Toulouse. Crusaders on their way home from Constantinople and Palestine who disembarked at Fréjus and Marseilles could not help seeing a strange resemblance between the dark, thin southerners, with their prominent bones and long faces, and the infidels they had fought with such pious enthusiasm and thirst for pillage.

It was true that the barons of Provence and Gascony had been their comrades. But as they ascended the Rhone on their way to the forests of Brittany or the plains of Flanders, they saw towns the architecture of which differed from that of their own, towns which from a distance bore a resemblance to those which they had just been besieging, and before which so many avaricious knights had fallen, for a booty that was inadequate. They saw the hated relics of the Saracen invasion. Not far from Saint-Tropez lay the mighty bulk of the château of Fraxinet, from which the infidels had for so long commanded the Mediterranean coast; there were also the turreted fortifications of Narbonne; the abbey of Saint-Donat near Grenoble; and the octagonal hill-towers which guarded passes and cross-roads and bore witness to the invasion of the Moors from Spain. The dresses of the women were too ostentatious, and there was something Oriental and immodest about them. The language had a barbarous resonance. The towns contained a great number of Jews, who not only were completely free to practise their religion, but had prosperous businesses or professed letters or medicine, and were honoured by the nobles.

When, therefore, at the order of Pope Innocent III, the monks of Citeaux scattered all over France to preach the war of extermination against Raymond VI, Count of Toulouse, and the whole of the south, they found the ground prepared. The campaign offered a thousand times as many advantages as that on which they had ventured overseas on the pretext of freeing the tomb of Christ. The Church offered the same spiritual advantages, redemption of sin and even eternal life ; while the material advantages were immediate and familiar. The châteaux were rich, the women beautiful, the wine abundant. It was assuredly a task blessed by God to invade this country, which was brown like Palestine ; to kill these turbulent, rebellious men of Oc ; to possess, in a setting of Moorish fabrics, their wives, who were as perverse as daughters of Satan.

Three terrible figures dominate the great Albigensian massacre. For the massacre to be possible, it was necessary that an extraordinary genius for violence, for organisation, and for hypocrisy, should take shape in three men, who were all equally devoid of pity and, possibly, equally sincere in their hatred of heresy and love of the Church.

It was Pope Innocent III who, with obstinate determination, desired and decided on the crusade. The murder of the papal legate Pierre de Castelnau was only a pretext. Historians are unanimous in gloryifing this pope. To them the great men of history are men who do something, who have a powerful will and exert it to attain an aim. It makes no difference whether the aim is sublime or abominable; it is success in attaining the aim which gives the measure of genius.

As soon as he was elected pope, in all his public utterances Innocent III began to talk of "exterminating the impious." It was the dominating idea of his life, and he realised it wholeheartedly. He had a deep-rooted conviction that any man who attempted to build up a personal view of God which conflicted with the dogma of the Church must be burned without pity at the stake.

He went even farther. He considered it his duty to exhume the bodies of dead heretics whose heresy was unknown during their lifetime, in order to deprive them of a peace to which they had no right. In 1206 he excommunicated an abbot of Faenza who refused to allow the exhumation of the body of a heretic buried in the abbey cemetery. "Skilful enquiry by Catholics," he said, "must bring to light the crime of those who have pretended to lead a Christian life in order to deceive public opinion."

In a decree to the citizens of Viterbo he assured them that "the divine sentence punishes fathers in their sons, and the canonical laws sanction this disposition."

Though he was thoroughly well informed as to the moral purity of the Albigenses and the Catharists, he spoke of them as "lascivious sects, who, overflowing with libertine ardour, are but slaves to the pleasures of the flesh." He exhorted his envoys unscrupulously to betray the Comte de Toulouse by making promises which they had no intention of keeping, for in so just a cause as the destruction of heretics all means seemed to him good.

In Simon de Montfort* he found the iron instrument to serve his apostolic fury.

Simon de Montfort was a fortuneless soldier of noble birth. He was a man of sixty when the crusade began and was not attracted by women, a trait which may cause the commander of an army to show mercy when it is intended to massacre the entire population of a town. He was a man of austere morals. He was unable to read and had no desire to learn. Possibly also he would have been unable to learn. He was amazingly short-sighted: in battle he could hardly see the opponent he was striking. He used his sword entirely at random, and after the battle was over he would laugh noisily with his knights over the fact that he had been able to kill without seeing. He had a habit of keeping his eyes shut, and so was sometimes called the blind knight. It may be that some of his cruelty was due to the fact that he was never able to see the expression of despair on the face of his victim. He obeyed the pope's orders blindly. He was animated by incredible cupidity, though he was open-handed with the clergy. He could see no farther than his nose, but he had the gift of seeing riches through walls; by the time he had passed through a town he knew perfectly well which of the inhabitants it was necessary to accuse of heresy in order to confiscate their property, to his own profit. He was unconscious of the existence of the chivalrous code of his day. He seemed to be possessed by a fury of destruction, by a cold passion for razing castles to the ground, putting his prisoners to death, spreading devastation. During the ten years

* Father of the Simon de Montfort famous in English history.—*Trans.*

that the war lasted, on no single occasion did he show a streak of pity. He was devoured with hatred for the country which he was in process of conquering and of which he had been appointed ruler. He showed no love even for his own men. When he raised the siege of Toulouse he left his wounded behind him, though he could perfectly well have taken them with him. He was merciless to the humble, sycophantic to the powerful. He was the valet of bishops, the slave of the pope. A lion was his heraldic emblem, and certainly nothing so well symbolises evil as the features of that savage animal. He had the courage given by the knowledge that he was the strongest. He was the symbol of the evil that is incarnate in man, and that evil was manifested in circumstances that were the more terrible in that he wore the mask of the Archangel Michael.*

Behind de Montfort's head a saint raises a cross, as though to provide him with a halo and allow him to draw from a religious source his marvellous capacity for destroying towns and killing men. This saint was the Spaniard Dominic de Guzman. He represented in the spiritual domain what de Montfort represented in the earthly. But the enemy he was attacking had greater powers of resistance than the walls of Carcassonne or the château of Narbonne. His enemy was the hydra of heresy, which he saw hidden in men's souls. To gain his ends he imitated the Albigenses, went barefoot on the southern

* Michelet, trying to find some virtue in him, speaks of "his courage, his austere morals, his unwavering belief in God." He also tells with admiration the story that is told by all the chroniclers, of how he once helped his soldiers at the peril of his life to cross a river. M. Achille Luchaire speaks of him as "a resourceful diplomatist and a skilful organiser of conquered countries."

roads, begging his bread, eager to preach and to convert. His faith was as absolute, his disinterestedness as perfect, as those of his enemies. But he could not beg. He did so arrogantly and longed to strike with his stick anyone who, though he might have filled his wallet generously, remained dumb when mention was made of Holy Church. The men he met in the course of his wanderings had skulls as hard as his own Spanish skull, and in his fury at the impossibility of converting them he forged the plan of instituting a terrible Order, which a little later would convert by force. The sound of his voice was raucous, and he was never able to rid himself of his Spanish accent. On the French side of the Pyrenees men's voices are musical, and a southerner knows his own race by a light in the dark eyes which the monk of Osna did not possess. He had not the capacity for winning hearts. He felt that he was among his kin only when he was once more in the presence of the northern barons. Simon de Montfort never acted without taking counsel with him. And the mystic followed the soldier. He never uttered a word in favour of mercy. He never intervened on behalf of the wives or children of heretics who were to be burned in his sight, and he was present at every butchery. Moreover he regarded the evils of the crusade as just punishment for sins which deserved no pardon. He said to the crowd at Prouille :

"Where you heed not the blessing of the Church, you shall heed the stick. We will stir up against you princes and prelates. Towers shall be destroyed and walls broken down, and you shall be reduced to slavery."

He had no scruple about taking possession of houses

stolen from barons of the south and given him by de Montfort for use as monasteries of his Order. A ball of fire miraculously falling at night on the demesne of Prouille indicated to him God's wish that there should rise there the school of proselytisers which was to bear his name; and he had no hesitation in dispossessing Guilhem de Prouille of his family property. His disciples after him glorified the saint and were elated by the miracle; they did not regard it as improbable that God should have sent a ball of fire in order to designate the scene of a theft.

The trend of his life is indicated by another miracle which took place at Toulouse in 1234, on the day of his canonisation. Bishop Raymond had just celebrated the canonisation in the Dominican convent. As he was on his way to the refectory to consummate the religious ceremony by a feast, word was brought him that a heretic woman of Toulouse lay at the point of death in the rue de l'Olmet awaiting the Catharist bishop to receive the *consolamentum* at his hands. Raymond immediately rushed out with his soldiers. The friends of the dying woman cried out, "Here is the Bishop!" The woman was misled and thought they meant the Catharist bishop. Joyfully therefore she affirmed her faith to Raymond, answered all his questions, gave him the names of the believers whom she knew. The Bishop and the Dominicans quickly had her condemned, and they had just time to watch her burning in the market-place near by without being obliged to postpone their feast. But the woman's happy blunder and the swiftly kindled stake were signs of St Dominic's favour. The monks returned to the refectory singing canticles to celebrate the miracle which signalised the canonisation of the saint.

The history of the Albigensian crusade is, or rather ought to be, well known. I will summarise it briefly.

Catharism was spreading with extraordinary speed in Southern France. It was the radiant cult of the pure spirit which took possession of men's souls, and it seriously endangered the materialistic Church of the pope. Innocent III realised this and despatched several apostolic legates to Southern France. These legates went to Toulouse, which was the capital of Catharism. They were resolved to strike a resounding blow, which should bring misery and terror to the south.

There lived at that time in Toulouse, in the rue du Taur, a venerable old man named Pierre Maurand, who had been the host of Nicetas* and held nocturnal meetings at which he preached the new religion. He was compared to St John on account of his shining eyes. He was a *capitoul* (magistrate) and one of the richest men in Toulouse. The legates summoned him solemnly before the people, interrogated him, convicted him of heresy and condemned him to death. The strength of a martyr was not in him. He feared death, which is usually harder to a rich old man than to other men, and promised to return to the Roman Catholic Church. But his return was made difficult. He was compelled to walk barefoot from the prison to the church of Saint-Sernin between the Bishop of Toulouse and one of the legates, who beat him unmercifully with rods. At the church he asked pardon on his knees, recanted, and listened to his sentence, which was that he should have his houses

* See p. 49.

destroyed and his property confiscated. He had, further, to go to the Holy Land and for three years to devote himself to the succour of the poor of Jerusalem. Before his departure, moreover, in order that no inhabitant of Toulouse should remain in ignorance of his recantation, he was obliged for forty days to visit every church in Toulouse, scourging himself meanwhile.

Pierre Maurand, who was then eighty years old, scourged himself and wandered naked about the streets for the prescribed forty days. After that he left Toulouse, crossed the sea and came to the East. He visited Arabia to discuss mystical subjects with the Persian Sufi, Farid Uddin, stayed in Tripoli, learned about the Maimonid philosophy, spent the three years in Jerusalem and returned to Toulouse, where his friends had never thought to see him again. His career was not yet at an end. It was hardly more than beginning. Typical of the stubborn men of Toulouse, he started once more preaching secretly, and for five consecutive periods of three years he was elected consul of the town by his fellow-citizens, who desired to honour in him the national resistance to a foreign pope.

People had grown so used to the idea that death could not take him that it was thought for a long time that he had taken refuge in the forests of Comminges; and a century and a half later inhabitants of the outskirts of Toulouse claimed to have seen Pierre Maurand going the rounds of the ramparts to examine their strength, leaning on his stick and erect as ever.*

* Being unable to believe in this astonishing longevity, certain historians have wrongly asserted that the consul elected for the periods following his journey to Jerusalem was his son.

The south had been terrified by the condemnation of Pierre Maurand. A pope who dared lay hands on this noble old man must be the pope of evil. Catharism grew ; the churches were abandoned. A new Church came secretly into being, without buildings, without a hierarchy, without grand vestments. The voice of Dominic the Spaniard rang in vain in the public squares.

The legate Pierre de Castelnau started back discouraged for Rome. He was a former Abbot of Maguelonne. On the day he had been promoted by the Pope to the rank of legate he was struck, as though by an arrow, with insane arrogance. He clothed his guards in scarlet and himself put on a strange ecclesiastical uniform of gold lace. He had just excommunicated Raymond VI, Comte de Toulouse, and had united magistrates, notables and people firmly together by addressing the Comte in the terms of a letter of Innocent III :

" Pestilent and perverse man, tremble ! Thou art like the crows, which live on carrion. Impious, cruel and barbarous tyrant, art thou not ashamed to protect heretics ? "

The legate had threatened Toulouse with destruction and had assured the inhabitants that he would personally see to it that the ground where now rose the turrets of the ramparts should soon be ploughed fields.

A certain young man, whose name has not come down to us, felt keenly the insult put upon the town. He determined to punish the arrogant legate. He followed him to the Rhone, which must have been easy, owing to the gaudy uniforms of the guards. As Pierre de Castelnau was making ready at nightfall to cross the river near Fourques, the young man rushed at him and wounded him mortally with a lance. He succeeded in escaping to Beaucaire and reaching Toulouse, where he received no punishment for his act.

When Pope Innocent III heard of the death of his legate he held his chin in his hand and invoked St James of Compostela. But he did not content himself with that. He sent messages to all Christian kings. Every Catholic pulpit fulminated curses. The crusade against the Albigensian heretics was preached and a promise given that the rich towns of Languedoc should be pillaged. The nobility of France, at the head of German mercenaries, prepared to march south by the Rhone, the Velay and the Agenois.

The south might have resisted the north. If Raymond VI, the most powerful ruler in the west after the King of France, had collected his troops and come to an agreement with the heroic Trencavel, Vicomte de Béziers, victory would perhaps have been with him. But he was possessed more by love for women than love for his people. Even as a youth he roused the anger of his father by seducing his mistresses. He had just married, as his fifth wife, the beautiful Eleonora of Aragon, who was sixteen years old and whom her father had been obliged to keep shut up in a tower because of her amorous propensities. Raymond wanted to be allowed to enjoy this passionate creature in peace. An Albigensian at heart, he was beginning to grow accustomed to excommunications ; but he feared an open struggle with the Church. Possibly he had that relish for self-betrayal which is met with in certain men who are weakened by love of pleasure. Besides, nothing great could be expected of a man who had blear eyes and soft, fat hands which were always slightly moist. He made his submission to the pope, and was vile enough to guide the army of crusaders into the plains of the south and fight against those who had placed themselves under his protection.

The crusaders arrived before Béziers, where the population of the villages, fleeing before the invaders, had taken refuge. The town contained—counting all who had crowded into it—more than sixty thousand people. A great number of them had taken no part in the heretical movement and were orthodox Catholics. It was here, in the name of the Christian religion and through the fanaticism of one of the most venerated of popes, that there took place one of the most ferocious massacres in all history. But most of the historians make only a passing allusion to the capture of Béziers, which they regard as an event of no importance.

The gates were forced on the first day by the advance-guard of *ribauds*,* as they called the bands of brigands who accompanied the armies to pillage and to plunder the dead. The crusaders rushed in behind them. On the previous day a council of military leaders and papal legates had decided on the extermination of the entire population.

An ingenuous baron had asked how they were to distinguish Catholics from Catharists. The Abbé de Citeaux, no doubt checking the smile called up by this innocent remark, replied:

" Kill them all; God will know His own."

* From this word is derived the English word *ribald*.—*Trans.*

As the streets were full of dead and the doors of the houses were battered in, the people sought safety by taking refuge in the churches. The crusaders set fire to them. Twelve thousand people are said to have perished in the cathedral of Saint-Nazaire, the roof of which fell in on three sides simultaneously. The whole town was committed to the flames, and the soldiers of the pope surrounded the great pyre, killing all who attempted to escape.

"May God receive the souls of the dead in His Paradise!" says a pious chronicler after recounting the capture of Béziers.

The Abbé de Citeaux, in the letter which he wrote to the pope giving an account of the event, modestly reckoned the dead at barely twenty thousand.

The young Vicomte Trencavel, who was twenty-five years old, as brave as Roland and as handsome as the hero of a romance of chivalry, had shut himself up in his impregnable stronghold of Carcassonne. His skin was milk-white, he was astonishingly beardless, and he had blue, trusting eyes, which made him look like a child. He had a square head, which called to mind the towers which the Templars were putting up. He was unsuspicious to the point of absurdity, and extremely violent. At Béziers, not long before, he had cruelly avenged his father, who had been murdered by certain notables of the town. Not only did he kill these men but, hearing that their wives had taken some part in the matter, he forced them to marry the murderers of their husbands, men of low condition. His subjects had seen in this a fine example of firmness.

It was in vain that the crusade attacked the stone

towers and thick walls of Carcassonne with battering-rams, flights of arrows and undermining. The bravery of the besieged repulsed all attacks. Trencavel's courage became legendary. The northern barons felt that this inspired young man was the heart of Languedoc, and that for them to secure the victory the heart must be torn out. They made use of his heaven-sent credulity to destroy him. They invited him to enter the crusaders' camp unarmed, under the protection of Christ, who was represented by the Roman legates, in order to discuss conditions of possible peace. The confiding hero, incapable of suspecting an unprecedented piece of treachery, accepted the proposal in spite of the uneasiness of his comrades at arms, who besought him not to leave them. No sooner had he reached the tents which sheltered the flower of the nobility of France than he was seized and made prisoner.

All day they awaited him on the ramparts. When night came, the defenders of Carcassonne knew that they would not see their leader again. Moans of sorrow broke out, which spread from tower to tower, from street to street, until there arose in the darkness a mournful lament, the despair of the town at the loss of the heroic leader who typified its life.

It was the fifteenth of August, the day of the feast of the Assumption of the Virgin, patroness of the crusade. The night was very light. The besiegers thought that the distant outlines of the archers on guard gradually diminished in number and finally disappeared. The nocturnal lament died down and ceased and there fell on despairing Carcassonne an impressive silence. The assault was to be begun at sunrise. The fortress seemed dead, like a great stone tomb. Knights and soldiers moved forward carefully under their shields, suspecting a stratagem. They forced one of the silent gates, and when it fell they advanced slowly, paralysed with amazement, through the town, which was deserted and dumb, like a town in the Arabian Nights under the spell of an enchantment. Through the half-open windows they saw the interiors of the houses with their abandoned riches. At street corners dogs howled pitifully. Pieces of armour lay scattered on the ground, and riderless horses galloped about in all directions. At first the besiegers thought a miracle had been enacted. Soon they learned the truth.

Old Baron Pierre de Cabaret, a friend of Trencavel's, had had built some years before a broad underground passage leading from the dungeon of Carcassonne to his château of Cabardez in the Black Mountain. Soldiers, consuls, the entire town, had escaped during the night. The crusaders were able to find for their gallows and stakes a mere four or five hundred forgotten Catharists, crouching in cellars. These they made haste to hang and burn, though they felt defrauded at the smallness of the number.

The south was virtually conquered. Simon de Montfort was elected ruler of it and he remained to complete the suppression of the heresy, with his troops drawn from the Low Countries and Germany.

On the day following the election it was learned that Trencavel, Vicomte de Béziers, had died of illness in the prison in which he was confined. But it was known to the farthest limits of Christianity that de Montfort had had murdered the man whom he had just wrongfully dispossessed. However, a murder was a small thing when it was a question of heresy.

And the heresy was still rampant. Castles had to be captured one by one, siege after siege to be undertaken. At Minerve, near Narbonne, at Limoux, not far from the mountain of ruins and human remains which was now Béziers, at Pamiers and Mirepoix—everywhere Simon de Montfort hanged and burned heretics. The monks in the abbeys and the ecclesiastical functionaries of the towns turned to the northerner who was the papal emissary, while the Albigenses fled to the forests of the Pyrenees. The untiring army of crusaders marched along the Ariège and the Garonne and massacred the whole population of Lavaur, the beautiful châtelaine of which, Dona Geralda, was thrown alive down a well, in order that her death might be slow and worthy of her great sin.

"We exterminated them with unbounded joy," says the pious Pierre de Vaux de Cernay, the chronicler of the crusade, referring to this incident. He records that on another occasion the Albigenses "rushed forward to the stake, so perverse and obstinate were they in their malignancy."

One victim, and that perhaps the most coveted of all, escaped de Montfort's fury. This was the château of Cabardez with its three towers, built on a spur of the Black Mountain, in which Pierre de Cabaret and the defenders of Carcassonne had taken refuge. Pierre's wife was Brunissande, the most beautiful châtelaine in all Languedoc, whose beauty had been made known to the world through the songs of the troubadours. He had a daughter by a previous marriage, the fair-haired Nova, and a step-daughter, the dark Stephania of Sardinia, both of whom were renowned equally with Brunissande for their physical beauty and their culture. De Montfort's knights dreamed of these three young women confined in the château with the three towers. What a guerdon for the conquerors! Before their tents in the long evenings of the siege they had rich food for their lecherous imaginations. There must have been quarrels over it, they must have chosen and drawn lots. It was said that Brunissande had refused herself to her husband from the mystic chastity of a Catharist adept; and this was a further attraction. Nova's virginal youth was also an attraction, and the barbarous soldiers, accustomed to rape in the towns they had just captured, must have pictured their entry into the château of Cabardez as entry into a paradise of carnal pleasure. But this paradise of stone towering among rocks and trees held out behind its portcullises and drawbridges. The crusaders were at last compelled to raise the siege and return in long columns to the fields of Carcassonne. They had only caught a glimpse of a white dress on a rampart, an uncovered head among helmets of steel. Behind them they left the three women, inviolate, like symbols of pure beauty of the spirit, which to the brutish man remains eternally inaccessible.

The Comte de Toulouse had vainly sought aid from the King of France, the King of England, the Emperor of Germany, and had equally vainly prostrated himself weeping at the feet of the Pope. From his frequent association with women he had attained an extraordinary facility in weeping and kneeling. He realised at last that no act of self-humiliation would save him. The heresy was nothing but a pretext; it was his lands and cities that they coveted. Eventually he decided on resistance. It was too late. His barons were decimated. He had himself handed over to de Montfort the pick of his own side. At Toulouse Bishop Foulque had put to death ten thousand people accused of heresy. He had been a troubadour and was an unbelieving adventurer who found it wise as he grew old to take up the career in which he would amass riches most quickly. He was so eaten up with covetousness that it was said of him he was envious of Christ himself when he saw an altar that was too richly gilded. When he left Toulouse he excommunicated, for the tenth time in a few years, its Comte, its *capitouls* and its inhabitants.

Thanks to the heroism of its men and women, Toulouse was not taken by Simon de Montfort. Twice the crusading armies broke before its ramparts. "O Toulouse, nest of heretics and tabernacle of robbers!" cried Pierre de Vaux de Cernay, furious at the prolonged resistance of a town that refused to be destroyed.

The crusaders left the impregnable town to ravage Albi, the Quercy and Lauragais districts, and the comté of Foix. Time passed. Reinforcements arrived continually from the north. On one occasion it was ten thousand armed pilgrims from Germany, on another it was the Comte de Bar at the head of trained troops. From Hautpoul in the Black Mountain to Lavenalet in the Ariège district, Simon de Montfort marched untiring, followed by a retinue of bishops and prelates, destroying lovingly, patiently, methodically, as though in obedience to a mysterious ideal of death.

A great game was played at Muret, where the King of

Aragon had arrived with a large army to defend the Comte de Toulouse. The south awoke and hoped again. The King of Aragon was a great captain, and victory seemed certain. But de Montfort still won. He was under the protection of the god of battles. In those times and in that country materialist man was bound to conquer the spirit.

At last, under the walls of Toulouse, which he was once more besieging and in which old men, women, and even children had now been armed, the invincible fell. A stone thrown by a mangonel in charge of a girl shattered the skull of the iron soldier, the man without pity. The name of the girl is unknown. A picture in a room in the Capitole at Toulouse represents her in the act of launching the stone that was to liberate Toulouse. Her face is not shown in the picture, for it has pleased fate that it should remain unknown. But in the movement of her arm and neck and bust, in the tresses of her hair, one can feel the courage, the mysticism and the independence of the southern race which was so unrighteously crushed in the thirteenth century.

Simon de Montfort's body was piously brought back by his son and brother through the country about Toulouse, Albi and Quercy, through the Black Mountain. From abbey to abbey, from church to church, the funeral procession made its way through silent towns, on roads from which the peasants fled when they recognised the banner with the accursed emblem. Now and again in a defile a stone thrown from a height would fall on the coffin as evidence of the people's hatred. At night in the monasteries where the body was received candles were lit and funeral chants sung. But in the houses round about all lights were put out. Simon de Montfort was at last leaving the land whose scourge he had been. The pope's terrible paladin was brought back to Montfort l'Amaury, to the monastery of Hautes Bruyères. On his sarcophagus was sculptured the symbolical lion, the ravening, rampant beast, with the inscription, *Most glorious martyr of Jesus Christ.*

Six centuries later the Revolution destroyed the sarcophagus and the sculptured lion, that the wind might carry his dust to the Pyrenees.

THE TWO ESCLARMONDES

MOVEMENTS of the spirit are almost always incarnate in a beautiful woman, who becomes the living symbol of them. The heroine of the south, the symbolical châtelaine of the mountain in the Pyrenees where the last Catharists took refuge and died, was named Esclarmonde. And since resistance was long and extended over a century, and since death was slow, there were two Esclarmondes. There was Esclarmonde de Foix, the chaste, she of the châteaux, who became a sort of high priestess of Catharism ; and there was Esclarmonde d'Alion, the bastard, *l'amoureuse*, she of the forests, of the Capsir mountain, who wandered with the hunted Albigenses, fought like a man, loved like a woman and died with those she loved.

Esclarmonde de Foix had given herself up since her youth to Catharist purity. She had sworn to devote herself to the spirit. This vow dated from her twelfth year. In the château of her father, Roger Bernard de Foix, she had seen the Bulgarian Nicetas, who was journeying through the south to bring the teaching of the East. She had had no opportunity of hearing him speak. He had only given her one look, and at the same time made a slight sign with his hand. Had he recognised in this silent child her who was born for the understanding and defence of the truth ? Esclarmonde was to remember all her life the flashing look that the messenger Nicetas had given her.

But before she became the apostle, the organiser and the soul of Catharism, she was to undergo a long martyrdom. Her father used his daughters as a commercial means of aggrandising his baronial house. He gave Esclarmonde in marriage to Jordan, Vicomte de Gimoez, a brutal soldier who laughed at the new mysticism and took the innocent girl in order that she might be the obedient instrument of his pleasures after hunting. Esclarmonde submitted to the violation which for men is sanctified by the sacrament of marriage; and it was only after her husband's death that she began an apostolate which was to last thirty years. Her conversion to Catharism was marked by some display in order to make an impression on the people. She leagued all the barons of the Pyrenees against the authority of the Roman pontiff and the local tyranny of the abbeys. She spoke, applied the religion of the spirit, became Esclarmonde the learned.

Legend gathered about her, and those who did not know her created an image of her, for a high ideal must assume a physical body, become living and active among men. When the Albigensian martyrs of Avignonnet, Lavaur or Pamiers mounted the stake and felt the flames licking their feet, they found happiness in the thought that somewhere, in a distant fortress among the Pyrenees, on the tower of Montségur amid the clouds, a beautiful châtelaine, clad in white, raised her hands towards the sun and symbolised the perfect purity of their faith.

Foreseeing the future and the defeat of the south,

Esclarmonde in her prudence had had built, as a last asylum, a final refuge, for the fleeing Catharists the impregnable château of Montségur, above the rocky valleys, above the silvery torrents and the pine-clad mountains. It was to Montségur that there travelled at night by remote paths all who would not deny their faith, all who escaped the massacres of the pious soldiers of the Church, the denunciation of the monks and the subterranean dungeons of the Inquisition.

For the avenging stone that had shattered de Montfort's skull gave back Toulouse to its magistrates and lord only for a short time. The day of municipal freedom for the towns of the south had passed. The Kings of France stole Languedoc from the Comtes de Toulouse; the bishops of the pope returned to their fortified sees, riding caparisoned horses and followed by retinues of Roman prelates. The tribunal created by the Inquisition for the express purpose of bringing to light hidden heresy, and composed of merciless Dominicans, began to operate in all the towns.

The story is so appalling that it becomes incredible, and it is hard to explain the oblivion into which it has fallen. The great barons in terror returned to the religion of Rome—the religion which never pardons any deviation from its intangible dogma—and delivered up their own subjects to the Church.

The Comte de Toulouse went to Notre Dame and there scourged himself in order to show his fidelity to the Church and the King. But that was not enough. Cardinal de Saint-Ange, the Roman legate and lover of Queen Blanche of Castille, dragged him off to Toulouse in order that he might kneel at his, the Cardinal's, feet in a ceremony of humiliation before the cathedral. At the same time he removed many professors, with the idea of reorganising the too independent university of the capital of Languedoc and giving instruction to the Toulousains in theocratic law, in the stern Roman theology and in the harsh dialect of Picardy and Beauce, which was then spoken in Paris, in place of the pure language of the troubadours.* It was not enough to take the maize fields, the blue vineyards and the beautiful houses with their Saracen architecture; the brains of these rebels had to be altered, their thought had to conform to the icy rigidity of Roman thought.

At Toulouse they battered down the profane symbols which adorned the façades of houses, and at Narbonne, opposite the château and on the site of the house in which St. Dominic had lived, they built the palace of the Inquisition. The presence of a miraculous fig tree planted by the saint intensified the fervour of the Inquisitors. The portal of this palace still exists; in the stone of the pediment a bucolically-minded sculptor, who had no doubt come from Italy in the suite of the legates, has carved some pretty bunches of lilies and a dove carrying an olive branch.

As a result, no doubt, of eating of the fruit of the miraculous fig tree the Inquisitors did their work thoroughly. The existing prisons proved inadequate and it was necessary to undertake elaborate building operations in every quarter of the town. In the Place du Peyrou and the Place d'Arnaud Bernard gallows were put up every day, and since the executioners were few and inefficient, others were sent for to Paris. Sometimes

* Napoléon Peyrat, *Histoire des Albigeois.*

a citizen disappeared and was never seen again. He had been immured. Men were imprisoned on the slightest suspicion of heresy. Denunciation, even when it had no basis whatever, was invariably taken as genuine. Torture was introduced into the procedure as a legal means of obtaining confessions. At this innovation a shiver of terror passed through the peaceful population of Languedoc; but the result was extraordinary. Confessions increased to an extent which exceeded the hopes of the judges. Everyone was a heretic. It was enough to have heard once in thirty years a sermon preached by an Albigensian preacher, for a man to be arrested and compelled, if necessary by torture, to search his memory for the names of those in whose company he had heard the sermon, perhaps thirty years before.

Human cowardice multiplied the treacheries and the denunciations. An Albigensian adept* denounced all who had given him shelter in his flight between Toulouse and Marseilles; the stages had been numerous and his hosts hospitable and charitable. Men passed through the town on their knees to ask pardon before the palace of the Inquisition for a heresy to which they had never adhered; they could no longer bear the terror of being suspect. Even the dead could be suspected and judged. They were solemnly exhumed, and the property of their children and grand-children—even though they were good Catholics—was confiscated on the ground that they had no right to what had been acquired by a heretic.

* The two chief grades in the Albigensian movement were denoted by the Latin words *perfecti* (" perfect men ") and *credentes* (" believers "). To avoid clumsiness the former word has been translated " adepts." See p. 97.—*Trans.*

The period during which the greatest number of stakes was erected and the greatest number of citizens immured was that of the celebration in Paris of the marriage of St Louis, the model king. The terror cut short commercial transactions, marriages, friendships. At Albi and Castelnaudary men were imprisoned because they were pale and were therefore suspected of practising Catharist asceticism, the rules of which forbade wine and meat. In order to escape this suspicion some of them rouged their faces when they went out and shammed drunkenness.

In 1245 the citizens of the towns addressed a complaint to the pope; the bishops of Languedoc, therefore, in order to counteract the effect of this complaint, or possibly from a ferocious sense of humour, complained in their turn of the excessive indulgence of the Inquisitors, whose laxity, they said, aggravated the heresy.

Despair fell on the population. Those who had in their heart of hearts retained the Albigensian faith had now nothing left to hope for from man.

MONTSÉGUR

IN the clouds of the Ariège mountains, like a celestial fortress, the château of Montségur, soundly built by the prudent Esclarmonde de Foix, held out impregnably against the armies of the king and the pope. The treasure of Catharism, its bishops and its adepts had found refuge there. In the mountains the barons and peasants who had remained faithful to the pure doctrine had formed themselves into armed bands, who lived wandering lives with the collusion of the peasants. The villagers had been terrorised into returning to Catholicism, but every man of them knew in his heart that the truth lay up there, with the last loyalists, in the depths of caves, beside the emerald torrents, on the slopes where the snow began.

Two generations had passed and Catharism still held firm. It clung to towns overhanging precipices, hid itself deep in forests, lit fires at night-time in the hills as friendly beacons to answer those on the towers of Montségur. There were epic fights in the mountains, unrevealed feats of heroism, martyrs whose names will never be known. It was the time when the solitary Saurimonde, the inspired prophetess of the Mazamet district, went naked as in the days when the world was born, because her soul was as bright as the sun that she invoked. It was the time when at Hautpoul, among the hills, Guilhem d'Aïrons healed the wounds of the

Catharists by stretching over them his hand with its magic virtue. It was the time when Guilhabert de Castres, the saint, moved about with strange swiftness to give the *consolamentum*, the extreme unction of the Catharist religion. He appeared everywhere when a member of the faith of the spirit was on the point of death. Dressed sometimes as a beggar, sometimes as a pilgrim, he appeared at the entrance of caves and in the streets of towns, in spite of the Inquisition guards and the watchers at the gates of the ramparts. When a man was being burned at the stake, he caught a glimpse of an adept hidden in the crowd making the mysterious sign of greeting, and died without suffering and comforted. For the love transferred from the one to the other had saved his soul and lodged it in its true habitation. And the elusive Guilhabert de Castres was always beside the stake to make the sign and transfer love to the martyr.

He died at a great age, and the greatest miracle was that he himself escaped the stake. Death, which for him was only the way that led to a better state, overtook him at Montségur. His bones were laid to rest in crypts that were so deep that the entrance to them could never be found and the Inquisitors could not exhume his body, to scatter to the winds his heretic dust.

By his side rested Esclarmonde de Foix, who had become a legendary figure, a silver-haired high-priestess. Her face had as many wrinkles as Catharism had martyrs. Her body was so withered that it seemed to be incorruptible. She resembled divine wisdom, which pierces its human envelope only to purify itself and rise in the scale of divine intelligences.

It was then that the second Esclarmonde, Esclarmonde

d'Alion the bastard, appeared. She was niece of the first Esclarmonde and daughter of Roger Ramon. One evening, her father, who was a bold hunter, lost his way as he was hunting a great wolf in the Ariège valleys. He killed the wolf, cut off its head and, as he was seeking somewhere to lodge for the night, caught sight of the gate of a convent hidden among the figs, myrtles and wild vines. He nailed the wolf's head to the gate, entered, supped and spent the night with the abbess, who was young, of noble family and beautiful. In the morning he left the convent. The abbess gave birth to twins : Loup de Foix, so called because of his father's exploit on the night he was conceived, and Esclarmonde, who was to become by her brother's side the heroine of the last of the Albigenses.

The supreme effort at resistance was made round Montségur, at So, Tarascon and Lavelanet. Esclarmonde was twenty years old. Before his death her father had given her in marriage to Bernard d'Alion, the seigneur of a small Pyrenean principality. She turned her château into a refuge for the Catharists and ordered that the drawbridges should be raised when the King's troops passed by. Her brother, Loup, was at the head of the rebels in the mountains ; she rode off to join him, clad in man's armour. She fought in the passes ; revictualled Montségur when it was under siege ; lit the night beacons which were the means of communication between the scattered groups of Albigenses ; with shepherds she pushed over rocks, which crushed the king's soldiers as they marched through gorges. Many a knight dreamed of this ardent girl, and as she overflowed with passion she gave herself to more than one of them, in the shade of the Pyrenean pines, beside her horse and her sword.

Montségur, resting on deep escarpments above its layers of granite, with its galleries opening on to precipices and its subterranean store-rooms; Montségur, which hid within its walls the tombs of its saints; whose towers bristled with the spears of its defenders—Montségur held out against the king, against the pope, against the curses of the Roman world.

Ramon de Perella was in command of the defenders. The barons who had been hunted from their feudal demesnes—men such as Lantar, Belissen, Caraman—took refuge there with their men-at-arms. Enough grain was stored there to last for years, and there were stables for horses and cells in which hermits prayed. Corridors plunged deep into the earth, and spiral staircases were cut in the great fortified rock. As at Toulouse, the women joined in the defence, for Montségur was the last refuge of the religion of the adepts.

A new crusade was decided on, and an army under the command of the Seneschal of Carcassonne and the Bishops of Albi and Narbonne blocked all the passes and valleys in the Ariège district. War engines of tremendous power had been sent for to batter the towers. Every day reinforcements arrived. Lavelanet was turned into a camp for chariots; spare ballistas were stored at Tarascon. The siege lasted for two years, and battles were fought every day.

Help came also to the besieged, for the Comte de Toulouse and the Comte de Foix, terrorised by the Roman Church, secretly protected the heretics. Once it was the son of the poet Pierre Vidal, a poet himself, who penetrated the enemy lines and made his way into Montségur to give good news. He had met on a road at night a phantom knight on horseback, wearing a purple cloak and sapphire gloves, which was a certain presage of the victory of the believers. Hardly had he brought them hope when he fell in combat. On another occasion it was Esclarmonde who forced her way in with a small body of men-at-arms. She soon left the fortress again, undertaking to bring away certain Catharist bishops.

But one by one the heroic defenders fell. They were now only a few hundred. From the depths of the gorge of the Ers or the valley of the Abès, the king's army could count them, on the high stone barbicans, in their battered armour, which still shone bright and with which the white robes of the adepts mingled. They had been told to wait. A great movement was making ready. The south was on the point of rising. The Comte de Toulouse was about to cease scourging himself and kissing the pope's feet. His troops were advancing on Montségur. "Only seven days more!" the messengers said. And on their towers they murmured, "Do you not see the army of Toulouse in the distance?"

But the army of Toulouse never came. Urged by a presentiment, Ramon de Perella removed the Catharist treasure at night, with a few men for escort, and hid it in the cave of Ornolhac. Some shepherds betrayed Montségur and revealed the narrow path by which the treasure had been taken. The soldiers of the Seneschal of Carcassonne, under the cover of darkness, penetrated into the Ers tower and forced the posterns. A general massacre was prevented only by a promise to surrender on the following morning. The Albigensian heretics had one night in which to take their farewells of one another, and when the sun rose over the mountains of Belestar they gave themselves up to the Catholic bishops. Pierre Roger de Mirepoix, who was in command of the combatants, alone obtained permission to leave the fortress armed and with his troops.

All the others were chained by the neck and led on to a great platform overlooking the Ers. A terrible stake was built up with oaks and beeches from the forest. The Bishop of Albi, in the kindness of his heart, offered imprisonment for life to all who recanted their heresy. Not one man accepted this offer. Priests and soldiers sang hymns as they hurled into the flames the three hundred adepts of Montségur.

The flames rose so red to heaven, the smoke so high and straight, that the men of Toulouse and Albi who were looking in the direction of the Ariège with anxious hearts, knew by this flaming sign that their heroic brothers had died and that the last hope of the south was extinguished.

The château of Montségur was destroyed. There was nothing left of it but calcined stones, save the name of Esclarmonde, which survived in the popular mind and in legend. Esclarmonde the chaste and Esclarmonde *l'amoureuse* were blended in a single person, Esclarmonde de Montségur. For long the villagers said they saw her wandering in the thick mists which rise at evening time from the steep banks of the Ers. After six centuries her presence is still felt in the ruins of the tower which faces the north. And it will always be felt there. Her hand may be seen above the clouds. It is making a sign which means that she is there, and that she will be displaced by no ecclesiastical tyranny, by no fury of dogma. For where the spirit has breathed it remains. Esclarmonde came to the Pyrenees to affirm that man must strive towards spiritual perfection, and that to show the way which leads there one can joyously sacrifice one's life.

THE CAVE OF ORNOLHAC

IN the Sabartez district, where the forests of Sarrelongue die down, there was a cave well known for its depth and its underground labyrinths. Its mouth was half-way up the mountain above the escarpments which dominate the Ariège at the point where the icy waters of that river receive the springs of Ussat. There the druids had celebrated their mysteries. The Saracens had halted there to sleep ; and there in their turn the Albigenses were to sleep.

Those of them who were still left alive were hunted in the mountains like wild beasts. Just as, later, there were officers in charge of wolf-hunting, so now special officers were set over the hunting of the Catharists and had at their disposal packs of trained hounds. The fugitives lived either in the plain among the undergrowth or in the mountains among the rocks. They lived in huts, which they had hurriedly to leave when there was news of the hunters. Sometimes they even took to the trees like monkeys.

A great many of these wanderers travelled in the direction of the cave of Ornolhac, in which it was known that the Catharist treasure had been hidden. There was formed there a new centre, a new Montségur. But this one was as deeply hidden under the ground as the other had been conspicuous above it. The untiring Inquisition was unable to leave in peace the dark hiding-place of these wretched men. By agreement with the seigneur of Castelverdun, to whom the land belonged, troops were sent under the Seneschal of Toulouse.

Legend relates that as these troops were advancing, Esclarmonde d'Alion—either from pure heroism or in order to share the fate of a man whom she loved—galloped along the bank of the Ariège and, when she reached the steep path which led to the cave, left her horse, climbed the winding track on foot and joined those of her faith.

The cave had two entrances, both of which were surrounded, but the Albigenses climbed ladders (which they then withdrew) to a yet deeper and more inaccessible cave. It seemed to the Seneschal of Toulouse impossible to attack them there. He thought it wiser and perhaps also more humane to substitute for torture and the stake a silent death in the darkness. He had both entrances solidly walled up. For some time he camped on the banks of the Ariège. He waited. He listened for some sound to reach him from the granite interior. Then he left the mountain which had become a tomb.

The Albigenses must have lived for some time in the darkness, for they had turned the cave into a granary. Several bishops and many adepts were among them. In the silent darkness the bishops no doubt uttered the words which promised divine pardon as a result of the imminence of death and of the liberation of the spirit. No doubt they stretched forth their hands over bowed heads in the invisible gesture of the *consolamentum*. And possibly as individuals and groups bade one another farewell in the darkness and Esclarmonde pressed close to her earthly lover, a miraculous light lit up the vault with its myriad hitherto lifeless crystals, the petrified oozings of the rock, the age-old stalactites. Possibly, by the miracle of love that joined them so closely, they attained all together, as it is taught in their religion, the abode where matter has no weight, water no fluidity, fire no heat, and where is enjoyed the blessedness of loving endlessly.

The mountain above the Ariège has kept the secret of the mass without candles, of the death without grave and winding-sheet. The book of Nicetas, which was kept among the treasure, the lovers' kiss, the bishops' gesture of blessing, must have petrified from absence of air. The last of the Albigenses, motionless, clothed in stone, still celebrate their final ritual amid dead vegetation and lustreless crystals in a basilica of darkness.

THE DOCTRINE OF THE SPIRIT

WHAT was the spiritual poison, the mortal error, against which the West rose in fury and which caused such torrents of blood to flow? The books in which the ancient truths were laid down, in which the tradition of the spirit had its written basis, were carefully destroyed down to the last page; so that we can recover Catharist ideas only in the bitter refutations, which are full of imprecation and menace, of the representatives of orthodoxy.

The mysterious Nicetas, before returning to the East and disappearing from the world to which he had brought a message, seems to have left a written memorial of his doctrine. The manuscript was no doubt kept with the Catharist treasure in the château of Montségur, and it must now rest underground in the cave of Ornolhac, held in the skeleton arms of a faithful guardian.

At the end of the thirteenth century a certain Ramon Fort de Caraman had in his possession one of the sacred books of the Albigenses. Feeling his life endangered by the possession of this book, he handed it over to the seigneur of Cambiac, whose wife was an ardent Catholic and a treacherous woman. She immediately informed the Inquisitors, but when they came the book had disappeared. It was ascertained through torture that the book was in the hands of one Guilhem Viguier. Men were sent to his house to arrest him, but he was found dead, apparently by suicide. What had happened to the book? It escaped the rage of the Inquisition. None of those who had kept the book and preserved it from destruction was an Albigensian, for there were none of them left by that time. The radiant power of the doctrine had set free in the parchment leaves a living force which enabled the book to survive and create faithfulness in the hearts of those who possessed but could no longer understand it. For long it must have been preserved among the archives of some castle with walls blackened by the old sieges of the period of faith. But where is the book of Ramon Fort now?

Almost all authors who have studied the doctrine of the Albigenses have asserted, with the weighty authority afforded by the Roman prejudice and with the ignorance that makes a man invulnerable, that the Albigenses were either Manichæans or Catholic heresiarchs, such as the Christian religion has begotten in plenty. In this they are wrong.

In imprisoning, burning and massacring, the Roman Church was logical from its own point of view. History shows that it has always marked down for destruction everything that was not in accordance with its dogma. In the case of the Albigenses the Church was in the presence of a Western branch of the Asiatic tree, the flower of the ancient Vedas, the pure truth of the Orient. The Albigensian creed, which, after spreading through Southern France, might have extended its tolerance and purity to the whole of the West, but which was to be finally destroyed under the trees of the Pyrenees, was born under the fig tree of Kapilavastu, where the Buddha preached his reforms.

The Albigenses were Western Buddhists, who introduced a blend of Gnostic Christianity into the Oriental doctrine. How the words of Buddha could have traversed continents and fallen into the souls of the men of Languedoc is not known, nor does it greatly matter. Thought is so fluid that we can never be sure that it is not active—even though it has no apparent means of expression—by the mere fact that it has been thought, in virtue of some subtle quality which eludes us. Buddhism travelled across the world, and among the people of Languedoc, who were then more mystical than sensual, it was transformed into Catharism. It is probable that, after their great impulse towards the spirit, persecution and disaster altered them, caused them to deteriorate and reduced them to the materialism of the southerners of the present day.

For the Albigenses the origin of God was unknowable. For the Hindus, similarly, Brahma, the cause of causes, is enveloped in a six-fold veil and is inaccessible to human conception. At a given moment of time, men's souls, in virtue of a law of desire which Christians call original sin, become detached from the divine matrix, from the infinite spirit, and are incarnated in matter for pleasure and suffering. They begin a journey, in the course of which, after reaching the lowest point of materialisation, they will climb again stage by stage through the organised hierarchies of creation, towards the first source, the divine spirit, from which they have been detached.

This last part of their journey, the return to the divine, proceeds by means of successive reincarnations in imperfect human bodies. In each life it is our actions, our capacity for detachment, that cause us to rise more quickly or less quickly. The more desires we have, the more we give rein to our passions, the more we love the material —by so much do we retard our entrance into the kingdom of the spirit. It is through illusion that we regard happiness as consisting in the satisfaction of our senses. Every pleasure of the senses involves a counterpart of pain. Every physical gratification is like a step taken by a traveller who turns his back on his goal. The goal in this case is the return to the spirit and the enjoyment of infinite beatitude. It is that which is called Nirvana, which is not, as ignorant people assert, the annihilation of consciousness, but participation in the universal consciousness, or even something more subtle and inexpressible—a permanent state of love which can scarcely be described by the word *divine*. The means of attaining this state is escape from the illusory prison of our body, which creates seeming pleasures.

The Albigensian wisdom, like the Buddhist wisdom, offered a method of destroying the desire for life, escaping the law of reincarnation, returning within the compass of a single life into union with the spirit. It was a method of renunciation such as Buddha prescribed.

Within the sect there were several grades. Ordinary adherents, who recognised the truth of the principles, enunciated and defended them as best they could, but continued to lead a worldly life, were called believers (*credentes*). They corresponded to those who followed "the middle path," recommended by Buddha for ordinary men, for the majority of men, for all who were not inspired by the will for immediate liberation. Above the believers were the adepts (*perfecti*), who had sacrificed the life of the body for the life of the spirit. They had renounced all magnificence of dress, the holding of property, the pleasures of food, and even the pleasure of the possession of women. Through the *consolamentum*, the sign of purity made to the dying, these adepts were able to transmit the invisible help which allowed escape from the chain of re-births and opened the approach to the spiritual kingdom. The *consolamentum* was only an external symbol. The Albigensian adepts were heirs to a lost secret, a secret which came from the East and was known to the Gnostics and the early Christians. The basis of this secret was the transmission of the power of love. The gesture of the rite was the material and visible means of projecting this power. Behind it was hidden the spiritual gift, by which the soul was helped, was able to cross without suffering the narrow portal of death, to escape the shadows and become merged with the light.

Never has any people at any period been so deeply versed in magical rites concerning death. The *consolamentum* must have possessed a power that to us is quite inconceivable, a definite power which had been proved to the living; for it would not otherwise have been so rapidly propagated, it would not have become so popular. The inspiration of the dying must have been visible to the onlookers. And for mutual help while they were dying they had processes the knowledge of which is lost for ever.

In the Black Mountain, not far from Carcassonne, there was found a chamber, dating from the Albigensian period, containing skeletons. "They lay in a circle, with their heads at the centre and their feet at the circumference, like the spokes of a wheel."* Those who have studied magical rites will recognise in this posture of death a very ancient rite intended to facilitate the escape of the soul, to allow it to traverse the intermediate worlds by virtue of the impetus given by union.

The logical consequence of the Albigensian philosophy is that life is evil and that it is expedient to escape from the form in which we are confined. The principle of creation, God the Creator, is consequently evil, since He has created form, which is the cause of evil. He is the Jehovah of the Old Testament, angry, destructive, Who takes pleasure in punishment and revenge. The Albigenses saw in this terrible God the retrograde power of matter. Jesus Christ, the symbol of the Word, came to teach man the means of escaping from this God and returning to the Kingdom of Heaven. Certain of them affirmed that Jesus had no terrestrial existence, that he only came among men clothed in a spiritual body, and that the miracles recounted in the New Testament had a symbolical character and had been performed only on the spiritual plane. The blind were healed only of spiritual blindness, because they were blinded by sin. The tomb whence Lazarus rose from the dead was the dark abode in which man voluntarily imprisons himself.

The true cult of the Albigenses was the cult of the Holy Spirit, the divine Paraclete, that is to say, of the principle which enables the human spirit to attain the real world (of which our world is but the reverse side, the caricature), the invisible world, the world of pure light, "the permanent and unalterable city."

* N. Peyrat, *Histoire des Albigeois.*

The conclusions which might be drawn from this creed seemed, for all their strict logic, monstrous to men of the twelfth century, as they would seem monstrous to men of the twentieth. Suicide, to escape the evils of life, which were still further aggravated by the persecutions, was at least allowed, if it was not actually enjoined.

The Albigenses, like the Romans under the Empire, sought death gladly by opening their veins. But they were forbidden so to end their lives unless they had attained absolute calm, complete indifference, in order to escape in the beyond the agony involved by a death incurred in circumstances of agony. The executioners of the Inquisition often found Albigensian adepts lifeless in their cells, their white faces showing the reflection of the eternal light towards which they were journeying.

Among them women played an unexpected part. They were the equals of men, for the law of reincarnation makes no distinction of sex. The only limitation to this equality was that women were not allowed to preach. Marriage for them was odious, and the indissolubility of its bonds was not recognised. The union of a man and a woman must have no other sanction than that of their mutual love. Such a union, however, was forbidden to the adepts, who might not propagate the human race and so perpetuate suffering through enslavement to the body. Believers who were joined to one another in the flesh were not permitted to lose sight of the effort towards final liberation. Thus, in the south, sons of the noblest families often married, without any ritual, the lowest prostitutes, or girls living in the poorest parts of Toulouse, or camp-followers, in order to regenerate them, to lead them one step forward up the long path to perfection; for brotherly aid of this kind is the noblest mission a man can undertake on earth.

They had a horror of lying, and they pressed as far as the Hindus the prohibition against killing animals and eating their flesh. Yet they were unjust enough to except snakes from this prohibition, for one of their superstitions was to believe that evil often incarnated in reptiles, and that in no circumstances could the body of a reptile serve as a temporary body for a soul condemned to repent in animal form.

But what excited the greatest hatred of them was their contempt for the things of this world, their exaltation of poverty as an ideal. They did not recognise property; and however far back one goes in history it can be seen that the man who has renounced this essential tie and deprived himself with love in his heart, becomes an object of execration on account of the social danger he represents.

It was in imitation of the Albigenses that Dominic went barefoot along the roads begging, to fight them with their own weapons, unselfishness and poverty. St Francis and his order also imitated this example. But though asceticism may have been permitted to obedient monks within the Church, it was not permitted in the case of a race which practised it wholesale, and whose voice was loud enough to express its indignation at papal tyranny and kingly cupidity. A man had the right to rise towards God by meditation and asceticism if he was an obscure member of a monastery whose other members extorted tithes and taxes by agreement with the barons and the king. But if an entire race ceased to work and to produce children, no longer recognised the authority of their masters but obeyed an inner authority ; if they presumed to have dealings direct with God and disregard self-seeking intermediaries—that race must be exterminated. And this was done.

The principal cause of the great massacre of the Albigenses, the hidden cause but the true one, was that the ancient teaching of the mysteries, so jealously guarded by all priesthoods in every temple in the world, had been revealed. More than that. It had not only been revealed—it had also been understood. What happened at that time had never been known in the history of the universe. While the ecclesiastical guardians of the secret muttered the Latin ritual of its formulæ (the meaning of which they had lost), the divine secret itself had been carried by unknown messengers along the roads and ways of Languedoc, beside the clear waters of the Tarn and the Ariège. The humblest men had been dazzled by it, and they had laid down their sword or abandoned their plough to answer the call of God. For the universe of which they had just caught a glimpse was a thousand times more beautiful than their horizon of vines or their forest-covered valleys.

It was then that the faithless guardians realised that the gold of the tabernacles would grow dim, the splendour of the altars fade. They trembled as the Brahmins of India had trembled at a lesser danger, the Buddha's reforms ; as the fire-priests of Persia had trembled at Zoroaster's words.

Woe to those who possess themselves of the secret and divulge it ! The hierarchies of the Greek and Roman priests, supported by republics and emperors, also punished with death the disclosure of the mysteries. Never before had the mystery been so far unveiled for mankind. Never before had organised society, with its edifice of priests, barons and kings, been in such danger. The slaves were throwing off their slavery without destroying their masters' fortress, without a revolution; they were doing it effortlessly, naturally, by the mere play of their thought. Pope Innocent III and Philip Augustus must have had a vague consciousness that their dominion was compromised, that their thrones would thenceforward have no basis. The oppressed masses of the weak were escaping from the strong by a door leading to the beyond, which had been opened by an unknown hand.

The Albigensian war was the greatest turning-point in the religious history of humanity. When the labourer understands the vanity of labouring; when the beggar refuses alms because he is richer than the alms-giver; when the word of the priest becomes valueless to everyone because each man has a higher consolation within himself—then the social organisation crumbles of its own accord. The freedom which humanity so nearly came to know was far greater than the freedom of a conquered people throwing off its yoke. It was liberation from evil itself, from the overwhelming power of Nature. It spread with the speed of a fire among pines in summer. But the men who hated the light were stronger. Not contented with extinguishing the divine fire, they rushed upon any twig that might give light and heat, heaped ashes upon the smallest spark. They called to their aid their old ally, invincible ignorance, the friend of darkness. They did not allow the survival of a fragment of teaching, a page of a book, an inscription on a wall.

There was to be no trace left of the truth the Albigenses had discovered. Now, six centuries later, when men pride themselves on learning everything and knowing everything, history has actually passed by this light without re-kindling it. To us the Albigensian war is only the account of the birth and death of a heresy, a chapter superadded to the history of French unity.

The sublime secret of the *consolamentum*, which allowed a man to die cheerfully because he was identified by the inspiration of love with the God within him, has been for ever lost. Not a hill around Toulouse, not a mountain among the Pyrenees, has preserved a trace of the secret on its stone. Moreover, the veil of ignorance has fallen so thickly about men's souls that no one thinks of seeking it, no one even believes in the possibility of its existence.

FERROCAS' MAY-TREE

NAPOLÉON PEYRAT writes, in his *Histoire des Albigeois*, that when he visited the shepherds' village of Montségur, which is situated at the foot of the ruined château, he was struck by the sight of a tomb on the right of the road, surmounted by a plain iron cross. He questioned the guide who was conducting him and was told that it was the grave of a man named Ferrocas, who had died some years previously.

Ferrocas, whom the guide had himself known, was a solitary old peasant, a sort of rustic philosopher, who always refused to go to mass. The village priest had reproached him vehemently and had even denounced him in public from the pulpit. Ferrocas claimed to be the only man to practise the true religion, which was not the religion of the churches. He said familiarly that he bore the Christ within himself, that he discovered him a little more every day, and that he would succeed in finding him completely only much later, in a future life—words which were unintelligible to his listeners and gave him a reputation for insanity. When he died, the priest—a worthy man for all that—determined to make an example of him and refused permission for his body to be buried in the cemetery. The villagers of Montségur dug a hole at the roadside for the old philosopher, as though he had been a dog. But they chose a spot under a big white may-tree. Nature in her equity decided that the tree should flower profusely, should become a flowering arch. The priest in his turn died, but his successor, who was told the story of Ferrocas' impiety and who every day passed by the tomb overhung with flowers, had the may-tree cut down and put in its place the rude cross which Napoléon Peyrat saw. It was about the year 1860 that this historian, who was a lover of the south, visited Montségur and saw the cross.

There is no doubt that Ferrocas was the last of the Albigenses, who must have borne semi-consciously within himself the remnants of the doctrine for which his fathers had died. But it was written that the Catharists of Southern France should be persecuted in their creed down to the last man. It was only owing to the freedom of the century that Ferrocas' bones were not exhumed and scattered. His white may-tree was taken from him. His mortal remains still have to bear the weight of the cross in the name of which he once suffered and died.

Poor Ferrocas ! His fate was that of all southerners. When the great Albigensian movement was suppressed, the grandchildren and great-grandchildren of the heretics were compelled to wear a yellow cross a foot long, sewn on their clothes back and front, in order that their connection with the heresy might be known and the curse carried on in them. Civil employment and the right to trade were forbidden them. They were called *cagots*, and their conditions were assimilated to those of lepers. Like lepers, they had in every town a special street or quarter of their own ; they might only enter churches by a small door, and a chapel was reserved for them, because the stones touched by their feet were contaminated.

Nowadays the descendants of the Albigenses are not treated like lepers, nor are they compelled to wear a yellow cross on their breasts. It is because they have become like ordinary humanity. But they bear, all of them, a sign that is more to be feared than the yellow cross: the sign of ignorance. They have forgotten. They do not know. They have dissociated themselves from the sufferings of their forefathers. They learn vaguely the history of France, but they do not know the history of their own country. When the bell rings at Albi in the Tour de San Salvi, it awakens no echo. No one counts the dead of Pré-comtal, near Toulouse. When foreigners walk on the ramparts of Carcassonne with their dumb Baedekers under their arm and ask what that dust is on the horizon, no one answers them that it is the dust raised by the ghosts of de Montfort's army.

When I myself was twenty I came from Toulouse, where I was born, and walked with no emotion whatever down the slopes of the Castellar de Pamiers, where Esclarmonde de Foix had lived; I saw Mirepoix and Lavelanet; I walked on the roads where Esclarmonde d'Alion's horse had whinnied, completely unaware of the epic that had been enacted in this country. Of the Albigenses I knew only what one learns at school, that is to say, nothing more than their name, the glory of Simon de Montfort and the overthrow of Toulouse. I walked between Mont Bidorte and the forest of Belestar, among the chestnuts and the ferns, to the sound of sawmills and of water against the rocks. I saw in the distance the shadowy outline of the ruin that was Montségur; then, as the sun was about to set, I compared the distance with my tepid curiosity, and retraced my steps.

And so it is with all who have wished to study Catharism and its sublime philosophy. At the mass of illegible documents they lose heart and find the way too long. They catch a glimpse of the tower of Montségur in the distance, veiled in cloud, and give up the attempt to reach it.

I have to remember my own expedition in order to account for the oblivion into which an important part of history has fallen. And I sometimes wonder if it is not some deeper cause than the lack of legible documents that has estranged Western minds from the wisdom of the Catharist sect. When I see cultured southerners confusing their heroic forefathers with the Saracens, or even the Goths ; when I see learned students of the history of philosophy and religion passing over the Catharist doctrine—I begin to believe in a sort of conspiracy of silence, an organised attempt to suppress the truth.

But the truth cannot die, and when it is smothered in one place it springs up again a little later in another place, near by, in a nobler form. It is true that an iron cross by the roadside near Montségur still survives as the symbol of the spirit. But who will go to Montségur and plant another may-tree for Ferrocas in place of the cross ?

CHRISTIAN ROSENKREUTZ AND THE ROSICRUCIANS

THE LIFE AND TRAVELS OF CHRISTIAN ROSENKREUTZ

IN Southern France there are certain districts covered with pines which are periodically ravaged by fires. Often the pines grow again, and where before there was nothing but calcined dust you may see, some years later, a new forest of resinous trees. But sometimes, as though the violence of the fire had reached the very seeds themselves, the hill that was once covered with pines remains bald and barren. Then on the top of the hill there springs up a single tree, which, strangely full of life, rises solitary as though to attest the lost presence of a dead forest.

So of the great Albigensian forest, which was cut down, burned and reduced to ashes, there survived but one man, who was to perpetuate the doctrine by transforming it. Like the solitary pine on the hill, he plunged his vigorous thought deep into the human soil of his time and saw it rise high into the blue heaven of the centuries with its foliage of books.

From the Albigenses there sprang in the middle of the thirteenth century the wise man who is known under the symbolical name of Christian Rosenkreutz and who was the last descendant of the German family of Germelshausen.* There are no precise data here—only a

* Almost all who have made a study of the Rosicrucians fix—wrongly, in my opinion—the birth of Christian Rosenkreutz in the middle of the fourteenth century. Some even place it in the fifteenth.

tradition, a story told orally. There is no written text, no historical proof. How could there be? So intense was the desire to suppress the heresy that not only were the bodies of the heretics destroyed, but even the stones of the houses that had sheltered them, and the documents which might have enshrined their thought. Besides, these heretics very soon realised that their only chance of survival lay in wrapping themselves in obscurity, hiding under false names, corresponding in cipher. History can no longer be traced except under the disguise of legend. But a man who has left so deep a mark after a life so obscure and so lacking in wonders and miracles cannot have been created by legend. Discretion, modesty, unostentatious goodness, knowledge without parade—these are not the attributes of legend. Christian Rosenkreutz is as real a figure as Jesus or Buddha; their attributes may be more glorious, but their historical foundation is scarcely more secure.

The Albigensian doctrines had spread fragmentarily to the north of France, the Low Countries and Germany. Families of refugees had found their way there. Solitary men had escaped, begging their way, from the sunny land in which they were thenceforward outlaws and accursed. Many of them died. But some reached the distant countries where the vine does not grow, where the rivers are more rapid and the sun less hot. And some of them gave an account of what they had heard in their low houses under the shelter of the ramparts of Toulouse or in the shadow of Montségur; they imparted to others what was still a flaming truth in their hearts. A few of them were understood. Little nuclei of Albigenses formed round a preacher, a spare, brown-faced man, who looked like a Saracen. The seed carried by the wind was thus to germinate in the country to which chance had brought it.

Under the influence of a wandering Albigensian the doctrine crossed the fir-grown mountains and flowered in the Rhön district, on the border of Hesse and Thuringia. In the middle of the Thuringian forest stood the castle of Germelshausen. The men who inhabited it were a grim, sullen family, half-brigands, whose Christianity was mixed with pagan superstitions. They spent their time fighting their neighbours, and they did not disdain to ambush and rob travellers. They venerated an idol of worn stone, the origin of which was unknown to them. It was probably the fruit of some long-past pillaging expedition. It might have been a Greek statue of Athene. It stood in the courtyard of the castle beside the chapel door.

The period was the middle of the thirteenth century. Germany had just been devastated by the fanatical Dominican, Conrad of Marburg, the envoy of Pope Gregory IX. Another Dominican, Tors, carried on his work. He was accompanied by a one-eyed layman called Jean, who claimed that his single eye had been given the divine faculty of distinguishing at first glance a heretic from a good Christian. Almost all who came within the field of view of this terrible eye were marked with the mark of heresy. It was no doubt enough for him to catch a glimpse, through the rocks and firs, of the towers of the castle of Germelshausen to discover from the colour of its stone that it sheltered a brood of heretics. Perhaps something of the power of the eternal spirit was given off from the ancient statue that stood in the courtyard. Landgrave Conrad of Thuringia, who had razed to the ground the little town of Willnsdorf, decided on the destruction of the castle. He besieged it several times, at intervals of some years. The castle fell at last, and the whole family of Germelshausen (which now adhered to the mystical doctrine of the Albigenses, practised its austerities, and believed in reincarnation and in the *consolamentum*, which delivers from reincarnation) was put to death at the final assault.

The youngest son, who was then five years old, was carried from the burning castle by a monk who had taken up his quarters in the chapel and who had been struck by the amazing intelligence shown by the child. This monk, this ascetic dweller in the chapel of the Germelshausens, was an Albigensian adept from Languedoc, and it was he who had instructed the family. He took refuge in a monastery near by, into which the breath of heresy had already penetrated.

It was in this monastery that the last of the Germelshausens, who was to be known by the name of Christian Rosenkreutz, was brought up and educated. He learned Greek and Latin and, with four other monks of the community, formed a fraternal group determined to devote themselves to the search for truth. They made a plan to seek this truth at the source whence it had always sprung, the East.

Two of them started out, Christian Rosenkreutz, who was then fifteen, and one of the four monks whom the *Fama Fraternitatis** calls Brother P.A.L. The pretext

* The *Fama Fraternitatis* was published anonymously in the seventeenth century. It is a crude summary of all that was known at that time of the genuine Rosicrucians.

of their journey was a pilgrimage to the Holy Sepulchre. Their real aim was to reach a centre of initiation, and they no doubt had precise knowledge as to where it was to be found.

Brother P.A.L. died in Cyprus, where the hazards of travel had led the two companions. Christian continued his journey and, no doubt as a result of directions he had received, made for Damascus. He did so because the tie with the East, which was about to be broken, still existed. Just as Apollonius had learned from the Pythagorean groups among whom he lived the exact whereabouts of the *abode of wise men*, so Christian Rosenkreutz knew, probably from the adept who had instructed the Germelshausens, that Damascus lay on the path to initiation.

It cannot have been easy to leave the Christian kingdom of Cyprus for the country of the infidels. But to him who sincerely seeks truth all religions are alike ; and when he left Christian territory Rosenkreutz assumed the dress and appearance of a Mussulman pilgrim.

At that time Damascus was under the dominion of the Mamelukes. All the learned men and poets of Persia had taken refuge there from the invading Mongols under Hulagu. The destruction of Bagdad and Nichapur and the annihilation of their universities and libraries convinced the intellectuals of the East that thought was dying. There were rumours of the end of the world. There had been great earthquakes in Syria and a rain of scorpions in Mesopotamia. The Mongols occupied Persia and watchers on the ramparts of Damascus searched the horizon anxiously for the appearance of their advance-guards.

How great must have been Christian's astonishment in the city of the three hundred mosques, among men learned in the literature of the East! What discoveries for a young man so greedy for knowledge! He read the *Guide of the Erring*, by Maimonides; the *Alchemy of Happiness*, by Gazali; the *Golden Meadows*, by Mazoudi. He heard Omar Khayyam's poetry recited and made every effort to understand his books on algebra and Euclid. He discussed astronomy with the disciples of Nazir Eddin. He meditated on the *Masnavi*, the sacred book of the Sufis, and was amazed to find in it the mystical pantheism of his spiritual fathers the Albigenses. How barbarous Germany must have seemed to him amid the intellectual effervescence which surrounded him! In the presence of the great Arab civilisation now drawing to its close he understood still more clearly the necessity for his mission, which was to preserve the spirit and transmit it to the men of his race.

After several years' study at Damascus, when he had acquired the greatest sum of knowledge possible to a man whose sole aim is to learn, he thought to obtain a higher knowledge, for which he was then ripe. The enigmatic name of the place to which he directed his steps has been preserved by tradition. It was Damcar, in Arabia. At Damcar, which name probably designates a monastery in the sand, there was at that time, and possibly there still is, a centre of initiates. Damcar was for him what the *abode of wise men* was for Apollonius. He remained there some years, then went to Egypt, crossed the Mediterranean, visited Fez.

In the reign of Abou Said Othman there was in Fez, the city of the six hundred playing fountains, which was then at the height of its splendour, a school of astrology and magic. It had become secret since the persecutions of Abou Yusuf. It was there that Rosenkreutz learnt divination by the stars and certain laws which govern the hidden forces of Nature.

But he was eager now to return to his own country. He left Fez and took ship for Spain. It was probably at this time that he took the name of Rosenkreutz, which embodied the essence of his beliefs. He entered into relations with the *Alumbrados*, a secret society in Spain which had come into being under the influence of the Arabs, and which studied the sciences and practised a mysticism derived from that of the Neo-Platonists. They were engaged also in the search for the philosopher's stone in accordance with the writings of Artephius. This secret society was a little later to be wiped out by the Inquisition.

The *Fama Fraternitatis* recounts an echo of the disappointment experienced by Christian Rosenkreutz. He was anxious to communicate to others the new truths that he was bringing in the domain of science and philosophy. He hoped to set right mistakes, to transmit with love that which he had learned. He was received with scorn and laughter. In all times half-knowledge has enveloped pseudo-scholars in an illusion of certainty which prevents them receiving any new idea. Before a mediocre mind can grasp an unfamiliar truth, habituation is necessary, even though the truth be radiant as the sun.

It was then that Christian Rosenkreutz realised that only slowly can wisdom enter the human heart. He had to remember the persecutions that had struck down too precocious possessors of the truth. And, though he wondered at the time necessary for the spirit to develop, whereas a flower opens in a single day and a tree reaches its full height in a single century, he reconciled himself to leaving the acorns to the pigs and keeping the pearls for the elect, at the risk of occasionally mixing with the acorns an infinitesimally small amount of pearl dust. He considered the fine filters through which thought must trickle to the men of his race in rare, microscopic drops, so that they might not be consumed by it. He counted up how many he would be able to initiate and saw that their number could not be more than eight. He laid the foundations of an occult group which was so secret and the members of which were bound together by an oath that was so terrible, that the group was able subsequently to act as he had ordered, to pursue and attain its aims, for three centuries without its existence being known, except by vague whisperings.

The curiosity of superficial men who find pleasure in anecdotal history may have been disappointed by this secrecy. But who could maintain that it is due to the egoism of a superior minority scorning to enlighten their fellows and share their knowledge with them? How many men are there in Europe at the present day who are sufficiently free from intellectual pride to entertain an absolutely new idea? Is not this pride a barrier which precludes even the approach of a new idea? If Christian Rosenkreutz disembarked to-day from Fez and tried to explain that the problem of the unity of matter is linked with the development of love in man—would he not appear ridiculous to every academy in the world? If he tried to teach, would he not find, on the part of those who wish to learn, this incapacity to receive? To help him without hope of reward, would he find now, as he found then, even eight faithful monks?

Christian Rosenkreutz passed through France without leaving any trace. It must have been the time when the mystic Marguerite Porète was burned in Paris, and Christian was anxious to get back to Germany.

Long years had passed. Germany was affected by all sorts of mystical currents which sprang from the Albigensian heresy. There were the *Brothers of the Free Spirit*, who affirmed the vanity of external cults and sacraments, denied purgatory and hell, said that man was a fragment of God, which must, after a long series of lives, return at last to the divine essence. There were the *Friends of God*, who aimed at emancipation from desire, and were addicted to practices analogous to those of the Yoga system, while their philosophy was modelled closely on the Hindu theology. But the Church organised its persecution more intensely than these sects propagated themselves.

Christian Rosenkreutz, seeing the number of imprisonments and burnings, was compelled to weigh the danger into which the spiritual light brought those among whom it spread. He went back to Thuringia to find the three monks who had been the companions of his early studies. They formed a brotherhood of four members, and the number was increased a little later to eight. It was at this time that the brotherhood of the Rosicrucians had its greatest efflorescence and contained a greater number of true initiates than was ever again reached.

All the members of the brotherhood were Germans, except the brother designated by the *Fama Fraternitatis* under the initials I.A., who came from another country, probably Languedoc.

Christian Rosenkreutz first of all taught his disciples the secret writing and the symbols by which adepts corresponded with one another. He wrote for their use a book which was the synthesis of his philosophy and contained a summary of his scientific and medical knowledge. The rôle played by the brotherhood seems to have been to influence the few men in the West who were at that time interested in science, so that science might be turned in the direction of disinterestedness. It is possible that this was the great cross-road of our civilisation. If the aim of the Rosicrucians had been attained, science, instead of being organised for material ends only, might have been the source of a boundless development of the spirit. We have seen that it has not been so.

The men designated by the symbol of the rose and cross travelled all over the world, each one with a mission to fulfil. But with one exception nothing was ever heard of them again. Brother I.A., according to the *Fama*, returned to Southern France, where it may have been his task to rekindle the old Albigensian flame. But he must by that time have been very old. Did he succeed in resuscitating the sect with the same secrecy which surrounded the Rosicrucians ? Tradition reports only his death near Narbonne.

Historically, nothing is known of the activities of Rosenkreutz during the last part of his life, that is to say, at the beginning of the fourteenth century. It may, however, be supposed, without great fear of error, that he inspired Jean de Mechlin, who preached in High

Germany, and that at Brussels he was the source of truth from which the mystic Blömert drew. This inspired woman performed miraculous cures and published writings in which she taught the liberation of the being through love. Her disciples asserted that on either side of her they saw a seraph, who advised her.

It was in all probability Christian Rosenkreutz who was the mysterious visitor (as to whose identity so much has been written) of Johann Tauler. Johann Tauler was the most celebrated doctor of theology of his time. The learned world of Europe came to Strasburg to hear his sermons. One day he was visited by a layman whose name he never divulged and who converted him to a mystical philosophy, the ideal of which was absorption into the divine essence. For two years he kept silence and became a member of the sect of the Friends of God. This sect possessed the same characteristics as the Albigenses. It rejected as the expression of evil the cruel God of the Old Testament; it condemned marriage and taught poverty as a practical means of divine realisation.

Of the death of Christian Rosenkreutz nothing is known. As in the case of Apollonius of Tyana, no burial-place can be determined. It was a rule among the adepts to maintain secrecy with regard both to their birth and to their death. Was it merely to avoid the violation of the grave and the profanation of the body to which the Church condemned heretics? Or was it in some cases to permit the transference of their spirit into another human body, and to prevent even the suspicion of a secret so astounding to ordinary men?

There has come down to us nothing more than a

childish legend regarding the burial-place of Christian Rosenkreutz. Two and a half centuries after his death, at the time when the story of his life was beginning to become known, his disciples, or rather men who would have wished to be his disciples, asserted that they had found a geometrically-proportioned cave, in which rested, in artificial sunlight, the still intact body of the master.

In all times men have wished that those whom they considered greater than themselves should not die in the flesh. They attach less importance to the permanence of their spirit, although of course that is the only possible form of eternity for them. Thus, when the bodies of Catholic or Mussulman saints are found, they are said to emit a pleasant odour. But the true fragrance given off by the bodies of wise men in the silence of the earth and in corruption is made of no material quintessential atom, no perfumed volatilisation. The subtle radiations of their soul float over the places where they lie and impregnate them long after the bodies have ceased even to be dust. But you must yourself be a wise man to establish connection with this posthumous life; and if your perception allows you to catch a glimpse of the fact that the best cannot escape the law, it will also make you feel more deeply the sadness inherent in all changes.

TRUE AND FALSE ROSICRUCIANS

AT the beginning of the seventeenth century there broke out a sort of Rosicrucian mania. The *Fama Fraternitatis* and the *Confessio* published, in a naïve form, what ordinary men knew of the sect of Rosicrucians—which indeed was extremely little. A great many philosophers and scholars, as well as many impostors, attracted by the sublime philosophy of the Rosicrucians, claimed to be their followers. Secret societies were formed, which very soon ceased to be secret owing to the vanity of their members, who boasted of their membership. Most of these groups, when they were not Lutheran, bowed to the authority of the Church. Every alchemist called himself a Rosicrucian. Descartes tried to establish contact with the genuine brotherhood of Rosicrucians. He searched for them in the Low Countries and in Germany, but on his return to France said he had not been able to find out anything definite about them.

It has been asserted that Paracelsus, Francis Bacon and Spinoza were Rosicrucians; but there seems to be no proof of this. In the eighteenth century a new grade, that of the Rosicrucians, was introduced into Freemasonry by the Jesuits, who had made their way inside the movement and everywhere formed groups within it. The hardy independence of the heresies of the thirteenth century had disappeared. The so-called Rosicrucians recognised the sacraments, studied the Old Testament as the source of all truth, acknowledged the power of the Church and the infallibility of the pope. This is the line of development which all spiritual currents follow. The tree produces a beautiful flower, a perfect fruit, and falls a victim to an obscure force which poisons the sap and kills the tree.

But the true Rosicrucians carried on their work. Their brotherhood had never ceased to remain secret. Through the self-sought obscurity of each member no one ever knew the identity of those who belonged to the brotherhood. From the assertion of certain men that they were Rosicrucians the one sure inference was that they were not members of the sect founded by Christian Rosenkreutz. The influence of this free spirit was felt in the seventeenth and eighteenth centuries by all who struggled against the tyranny of Calvinism and Lutheranism, which were as intolerant as the Inquisition, and against the intransigence of the universities, which tried to submit all thought to the intellectual discipline of Aristotle. But the messengers remained faithful to their vow not to make themselves known. The message reached its destination, but it was not known who had brought it.

Certain characteristics in the lives of certain men may, however, give rise to the supposition that they were the true possessors of the Rosicrucian tradition. Paracelsus practised medicine gratuitously; his philosophy was Neo-Platonic; he wore only very unpretending clothes and exalted poverty; upon his appointment as professor of surgery by the senate of Bâle, he burned in the amphitheatre before the students the old medical books, which were believed in blindly but which, owing to the respect in which they were held, were actually an obstacle to research. Philalethes, who possessed the secret of the philosopher's stone, travelled all over the world to heal the sick ; his continual preoccupation was to escape the fame which his cures brought him. Although the Comte de Saint-Germain had a fondness for precious stones, he may, for other reasons, be numbered among the true Rosicrucians. But the same conclusion cannot be drawn in the case of Spinoza from the fact that his seal was in the form of a rose and that he did not sign his work. Certain too zealous writers have assigned to the Rosicrucians every remarkable figure of the last few centuries.

In 1888 Stanislas de Guaita and Papus founded a cabalistic order of the Rosy Cross, with a ceremonial, grades and, possibly, special dress. These facts, together with the stir which they made over this foundation, were sufficient indication that the new order was not inspired by the tradition of its original founder. The same may be said of the Catholic order of the Rosy Cross founded by Josephin Péladan at the same time. These orders had only an ephemeral life. At the present day there can still be found various groups, almost all of them Christian, calling themselves Rosicrucians ; but they do not correspond to any reality based on initiation.

The only true Rosicrucians, the eight heirs—who have followed one another in unbroken succession—of the Albigensian Christian von Germelshausen, have carried on their secret work uninterruptedly. Some have thought that towards the end of the seventeenth century before the growing materialism of Europe, as though they considered the game lost, they abandoned the races which were greedy only for material well-being and retired into the inaccessible solitudes of the Himalayas. But a game in which the stake is divine can never be lost. Possibly they left Europe at one time and have since returned. The legend of them, after providing one of the chief topics of conversation among European intellectuals, died down after the French Revolution. At the present day it interests only a small number of seekers after knowledge. The eight wise men have returned to their task, though this task has become excessive. By what means are they seeking to accomplish it ?

Sometimes it needs very little to turn a human soul in a new and better direction. It may happen that the reading of a book is enough, or a chance word that you hear—even the face of a good man that you catch a glimpse of one evening and that reminds you that good exists. Each one of us, when the moment has come or when he asks with sufficient intensity, may meet one of the eight wandering wise men. Let him not be in a bad temper that day, or inattentive, or tired. Wisdom is not capricious, as luck is ; but it visits us much less often.

THE ROSE AND THE CROSS

THE Rosicrucians took the union of the rose and the cross for their symbol because this union embodies the meaning of their effort and emphasises the fact that that effort must be made by all men. For immemorial ages the wisest among us have discovered that the aim of humanity on earth is to attain divine wisdom. Two ways lead to divine wisdom: knowledge and love.

The cross is the oldest symbol in the world. Ever since the appearance of the earliest civilisations it has denoted mind or spirit moving towards perfection. The rose symbolises love because by its perfume, colour and delicacy it is Nature's masterpiece of beauty, and beauty excites love, just as love transforms into beauty the elements on which it is bestowed. By the rose blooming in the middle of the cross the meaning of the universe is explained, the only true doctrine is summed up, the truth shines out with splendour. In order to realise his possibilities and become perfect, man must develop his capacity for love to the point of loving all creatures and all forms perceptible to his senses; he must enlarge his capacity for knowledge and understanding to the point of comprehending the laws that govern the world, and of being able to proceed, through the intelligence, from every effect to every cause.

He who breathes the perfume of the rose and savours

its beauty, who sees the branches of the cross open towards the four cardinal points of the spirit, may take the wrong road, may go backwards, may be for the time overwhelmed by ignorance. But he holds his anchorage in the storm, he sees the light on the hill-top; sooner or later he will once more find the right way. All glory to the messenger who found this safety-giving signal and fixed it in wood or stone that it might be transmitted! All glory to the messenger who, through the virtue of the symbol, created the possibility that the truth should be preserved! He has added name and number to the mile-stone; he has been the comfort of the traveller, the safety of the lost wanderer.

Christian Rosenkreutz made rules for his disciples' life. The first of these rules was unselfishness, which will always be the most difficult virtue to put into practice. The men who have a reputation for unselfishness and live among us with a vague halo of generosity, are only men who are less greedy than others. Nobody is unselfish. There is not a single example in our modern society of a man big enough to break the terrible bond of riches and pass readily and unostentatiously from wealth to poverty, or even from poverty to greater poverty. As soon as the mind has reached a certain level it understands that it is in this direction that the first step must be taken. Yet it does not take that step. One of the bravest men of all, and one most deeply convinced of the virtue of poverty —Tolstoy—made up his mind only a few hours before his death to become a wandering beggar. But he was too late.

Another essential rule was absence of pride. The Rosicrucian had to pass unnoticed, might not pride himself on his knowledge, had to remain so far as possible anonymous. For the ordinary man modesty is as impossible to practise as poverty. It is even a matter of common observation that great intellectual faculties are almost always accompanied by a form of stupid, boastful vanity. And this very vanity is regarded with favour as the sign of genius.

The third rule of the Rosicrucians was chastity. Wise men have always attached great importance to chastity, though neither Pythagoras nor Socrates nor Plato nor the Alexandrine philosophers practised it rigorously. Possibly it is nothing more than a preventive measure against excess and against the violence generated by such desires. Logically, if pleasure in eating is not forbidden there is no reason why the pleasure of sex should be forbidden. And these two orders of physical pleasures are in some degree comparable. In the ordinary man they are both equally indispensable to life. But while eating involves only the physical pleasure arising out of a good digestion, the other, if practised with a person who is loved, contains marvellous possibilities of pleasure and may even be a path to perfection. Only at present nothing is known of this path. The laws which teach how a high spiritual level may be attained through community of desire and its mutual satisfaction have not yet been written by any master. I have never heard even of there being any oral teaching on that subject. A prudishness that is as old as the world has cut short with a command of silence the forward impulse which humanity might have received through the flesh.

We do not, however, know whether the rose in the Rosicrucian symbol may not contain an implicit indication of the secret of love which remains to be found.

He who reaches higher knowledge through an enlarged intelligence will be able to love only those persons and things whose machinery he understands, whose movements he sees, whose passions he comprehends as though they were his own. He who reaches the state of perfect love through the emotional impetus of the heart will see the barriers of ignorance fall before him and will conquer knowledge by the bestowal of himself on that which he loves. For the two ways meet and at a certain level become one.

The symbol is well-founded and eternal, and there will be no need of any other for thousands of human evolutions. Every man can weigh himself up by reference to the rose and cross and can find in it a provisional touchstone of good and evil. It is the interrogation point which is formed in many consciences, though they may not confess it to themselves. What is good and what is evil? Am I right to do something which seems good from my point of view and evil from that of others? Naturally the rose and cross cannot serve as a key to every riddle, for there are too many doors in the darkness of the soul. The agonising question which every man asks himself at least once in his lifetime and most men ask themselves a thousand times, the question whether it is more important to develop oneself or to help others, whether it is better to sacrifice oneself or to progress by study, remains unsettled. But the two ever-present symbols give man the framework of an answer, if he is sincere with himself.

Whenever a man becomes identified through love with

that totality of universes which is called God, or with a landscape, or with some creature, though it be only a dog, he is on the way of the rose, protected by it and enriched by its substance. Whenever he emerges from his ignorance, learns a fact or a law, allows his mind to go a little farther in knowledge of reality, he is progressing towards that super-terrestrial and super-celestial point at which the cross stretches forth its four spiritual branches.

That is the message which Christian Rosenkreutz brought to the West. It is a message which may seem very modest to European sceptics (who are convinced that they possess all knowledge and consider hate more important than love). But it was brought very humbly by a messenger who gloried in concealing his name and who, after journeying for more than a century to transmit his little truth, has left no other trace of his passing than the design of the open flower at the centre of the cross.

THE MYSTERY OF THE TEMPLARS

THE INITIATES OF ACTION

IT was enjoined on the Knight Templar by the rules of his Order that he must never yield, but must contend to the last, with three enemies, if need be. It was commonly said, moreover, in the twelfth and thirteenth centuries, that a single Knight Templar could overcome ten Saracens.

The essential quality demanded of a member of the Order was courage, personal bravery ; and the sum of all this bravery was intended to establish the power of force, material domination.

The Templars were the initiates of action, the messengers of the sword. They signalised a fresh defeat to Eastern initiation in its work of bringing peace and culture to the West, which lay crushed in the embrace of the Church. At Athens and Alexandria the Church had previously annihilated the Neo-Platonic initiates of knowledge. The last survivors of that marvellous school, the disciples of Ammonius Saccas, who dreamed of leading the world to perfection through philosophic knowledge, had been compelled to take refuge in Persia with King Chosroes.

At the time when the Order of the Temple was attaining its zenith, the initiates of love, the Catharists and Albigenses, who had discovered the secret of immediate perfection to be attained in a single lifetime by the path of purifying poverty and brotherly love, had been exterminated to the last man; and from the Atlantic to the Mediterranean it was impossible to find a stone with the mark of their sublime tradition.

The initiates of the Order of the Temple sought to bring about by the sword the triumph of the truth of the sages. They followed the third of the ways open to man—not the way of knowledge or the way of love, but the way of action. Their initial success was dazzling. The flower of every country in the world, attracted by the ideal of chivalrous courage which they raised as a banner, joined them. Every high-spirited young man in Europe dreamed of taking his share in the defence of the Holy Land in the phalanx of these glorious veterans of the Crusade. But the directors of the Order had glimpses of a more grandiose aim. In their eyes the Holy Land contained the tomb only of a prophet among prophets, not of a God. It was their idea to make a Holy Land of the whole world. For this it was first necessary to conquer the world—which was within the bounds of possibility. The Order of the Temple made this attempt and might have been successful.

The eleventh and the twelfth centuries saw the development of this tremendous dream, this gigantic secret chimera, the conquest of Europe and Asia by a brave, well-organised minority, ignorant, however, of the real aim and directed by a small group of initiates. Success would have meant the re-establishment of the ancient

Egyptian hierarchy of priests. Behind the kings and their warriors there would have stood wise men, priests and scholars combined, who would have imposed a will to justice and turned the whole world towards perfection.

It is not surprising that in the rules of the Order no passages can be found testifying to this tremendous aim of the Templars. A project so vast as to include the fall of kings, the levelling of religions, and the setting up of a unique civilisation, which was to be both Mussulman and Christian, could not be entrusted to any parchment and could be revealed even to the Grand Priors of the Council only when their ambition and discretion had been carefully tested. At the time of the trial not a single knight revealed the true aim of the Order, of which he was but a blind instrument. The members of the inner group, those who knew, confessed under torture only external rites, which may have been scandalous to the profane, but which did not affect the essence of that which the Temple really was. No doubt Philippe le Bel and Pope Clement V were well aware of the danger to their throne and papacy. The extraordinary avarice of the King of France was not a sufficient lever with which to lift and break so heavy a stone as the Order of the Temple. It was possible that he would not succeed and would himself be broken. He must have decided on his daring course of action only because it was a vital matter for his throne. Not long before, he had sought admission to the Order and, to his great surprise, had been rejected. He therefore suppressed those who, a little later, would have suppressed him. The papacy would have been attacked only much later, for to attain dominion the Order needed the ecclesiastical organisation. At the trial, neither in the examinations nor in the judgments was the slightest hint given of the force which had all but destroyed the social edifice in order to reorganise it on a more perfect plan. It was considered enough to have convicted the Templars of having spat on the crucifix, of having permitted and even commended unnatural vice, of having worshipped the idol Baphomet—all matters which were proved in the letter, while the spirit was not understood. The astonished world saw the condemnation of the glorious and famous Order and never knew the real reason. And history ever afterwards has remained in equal ignorance.

The most prodigious actions can be accomplished by those who believe. Not only can faith move mountains ; it can toss them up to heaven with ease. Nor is it necessary that faith should be faith in good, in God, or in some sublime chimera. Faith in egoism has equal power. But it gives way quickly. However, the element of faith must necessarily be at the basis of action. When men cease to believe in their aim, their armour falls from them, they cease to be invincible. That is what happened to the Templars. The amassing of riches entered into their plan, and in an incredibly short time they had become the bankers of the world. The knights entrusted with accounts were even more zealous than those entrusted with fighting (and these had the reputation of being the best fighters of their time). Riches corrupted them as they corrupt all who possess them. They perished from their excessive wealth, and with them was extinguished the dream of a civilisation which should reconcile the East and the West, and for the rule of kings should substitute government by a chosen group of wise and just men.

HUGUES DES PAYENS AND THE ORDER OF ASSASSINS

IT was about 1120, in Jerusalem, that the magnificent dream appeared in the gifted brain of the founder of the Templars, Hugues des Payens.

He was a poor knight of Champagne who had followed Godefroy de Bouillon in the Crusade and remained in Jerusalem. Pillage had left him still without a fortune. History shows that when a town, however big, is captured, three days at most are enough to ensure that there is not a house left to take or a woman to violate. At Antioch and Jerusalem, Hugues des Payens must have spent the three first days in thanking God for the victory. It seems probable that the founder of the richest Order in Christendom was a disinterested man.

He considered himself a good Christian but liked to discuss heretic doctrines with his comrade-at-arms Geoffroy de Saint-Adhémar,* who came from Toulouse, and, like all his countrymen, was imbued with Catharism. They were young and poor, as is proper for the constructors of great plans, for men who swiftly transform dreams into realities.

The East, with the beauty of its architecture, the charm of its women and the mysticism of its philosophy, changed men of the West with surprising rapidity. Baldwin II, who had become King of Jerusalem, was

* Not *Saint-Omer*, as it is often written.

an example of this. Taken prisoner in an ambush by the Emir Balak, he had been for a year in the power of the Saracens. When he was set free he continued to fight with the same ardour, but he spoke of the Emir as a wise man from whose conversation he had derived much pleasure. He dressed in robes after the Oriental manner, affected their manner and married a girl who belonged to an old Arab family. He was the protector of the first Templars, to whom he gave as their lodging, perhaps with intention, that part of his palace which was built on the site of the Temple of Solomon.

Hugues des Payens and Geoffroy de Saint-Adhémar, who were at the same time combatants and mystics, were struck with admiration for that which the East was disclosing to them in the domain of ideas which interested them most. They heard nothing but stories of holy men of Islam who imposed their mystical conception by force. These men all used similar methods. They founded a secret society, which was both combatant and philosophic, with different degrees of initiation and a hierarchy of membership based on the hierarchy of nature, in accordance with the ancient principle: *As above, so below.*

In Persia there had been Mastek, Kermath and the Rawendis, who taught their initiates that souls transmigrate from body to body. The two Frenchmen heard also of "those who are clothed in white," of Mokanaa the masked man, who always wore a gold mask on his face, and of Sasendeimah, the "master of moonlight," so called because, to impress his disciples, he caused a dazzling light to appear above a fountain at night.

There was also the founder of an Ismaelite secret

society, Abdallah, son of Maimoun, who had succeeded in mounting the throne of the Caliphate of Egypt. Since his accession there had been in Cairo a society of wisdom, of which the Caliph was grand master. This society's " house of wisdom " and " house of knowledge " were full of astronomical instruments and books ; ink, parchment and pens were distributed free, and they were the resort of the doctors, the poets and the wise men of the East.

Hugues des Payens and Geoffroy de Saint-Adhémar heard at this period in Jerusalem the echo of a great event, the temporary closing, as the result of a riot, of the " house of knowledge " at Cairo ; they were amazed at the importance things of the mind seemed to have in the East, which they had actually thought barbarous, while they lived in their stone castles in the land of France, shut in by their gloomy moats.

The story of Hassan-ibn-Sabbah, the Old Man of the Mountain, and the sect of the Assassins, whose reign of terror extended over Persia, Syria and Egypt, and even over the Crusaders, was the subject of long talks during the hot Jerusalem nights.

Hassan-ibn-Sabbah, as well as being a mystic philosopher, was an ambitious man. Educated in the great university of Nishapur with the astronomer-poet Omar Khayyam and with Nizamolmouk, who was to become the prime minister of the Caliph of Bagdad, he had been initiated into the sect of the Ismaelites and had himself founded a sect, of which he proclaimed himself grand master. This sect had nine degrees of initiation and was based on the two foundations of absolute obedience and intellectual knowledge of philosophy. Disciples rose in the hierarchy of the sect according to their intelligence. After knowledge it was necessary to attain faith in the higher God common to all religions. On this level they practised the ecstasy of the Sufis and the saints. But on the highest level they were taught that there was for man neither reward nor punishment, that the world was governed by an indifferent law, and that individual egoism was probably the deciding principle of life. Only a few teachers of the sect reached this final degree. There must have been a still higher grade, which was reached by the first grand master, Hassan-ibn-Sabbah, and the agony involved in which he never revealed to anyone. On this level he must have had doubts of his own philosophy and of the final superiority of egoism. His disciples recount of him that he spent thirty-five years without leaving the library of the castle of Alamut, which contained so many books that it became the biggest in the world after the library of Bagdad. During this period of thirty-five years he was only twice seen on his balcony. But as a man who bore within himself absolute assurance he realised the vanity of books fully as much as a man of faith; he expected nothing from dusty parchments and he certainly would not have contented himself with seeing the sunlight twice in thirty-five years.

Hassan-ibn-Sabbah had found an ingenious way of becoming the most important person in the East, of raising taxes and controlling kings. Every man who resisted his will was assassinated by one of his emissaries. If the emissary was captured before he had accomplished the murder, another was sent, and if necessary a third. And Hassan's disciples stopped short at nothing. If it was necessary to kill a Christian they were converted to Christianity. Some of them disguised themselves as beautiful women and were sold as slaves in order to approach some suspicious, luxury-loving emir and stab him as he caressed them.

To turn his disciples into fanatics and obtain from them the sacrifice of their life, Hassan possessed a method of his own, which he bequeathed to his successors. Like his father, Ali Sabbah, who was surnamed the sceptic and atheist, and for whose attainments he had the deepest respect, he had made a study of plants since his childhood. He had found a way of preparing hashish and mixing it with henbane so that a man gained self-confidence and inflexible determination. His emissaries took with them, besides their short, triangular dagger, the absolute certainty of success. Possibly, as Marco Polo has told us—and all his other statements have received corroboration—Hassan gave his disciples another mixture of hashish which produced in them, by the fountains in the gardens of Alamut, blissful dreams and the belief that they were being sent to paradise through his divine power.* It was easy to obey a man who could give such a reward. It is from this fact that the members of the sect have derived their name of *assassins*, or *hashishins*, eaters of herbs. The Old Man of the Mountain was called the possessor of the Hashisha.†

* Part of the castle of Alamut was called Meimoun-diz, the fortress of happiness.

† Certain solemn persons are pleased to regard as unhistorical events which present themselves to us in the garb of legend. Facts are often flat and boring, but sometimes they are sublime and poetic without any embellishment. In his interesting work on chivalry M. Victor-Emile

At the moment when Hugues des Payens and Geoffroy de Saint-Adhémar were dreaming of power to be acquired in imitation of the Eastern intellectuals, Hassan-ibn-Sabbah died. But his sect lost nothing of its strength, thanks to the machinery of his organisation. The two Frenchmen had no difficulty in seeing that what gave it its power, more even than the dark threat of its daggers, was the methodical acquisition and fortification of impregnable strongholds, garrisoned by small bodies of disciplined troops.

And the dream took shape. It was possible to become master of Europe if one possessed castles scattered about various countries. To acquire these castles wealth was necessary, but religion led to everything, particularly to wealth. How many men had renounced their fortunes at the time of the Crusade, exchanging their money for the pardon of the Church! The knights of Christ would drain Christendom of gold. As regards the terror, the power of murder, which had been Hassan's principal lever, it could be re-created in a religious watchword, in the virtue given by faith.

This watchword came to them from the East through the initiation which they received from Theocletes, the Patriarch of the Gnostic sect of Johannites. This sect centred its beliefs round St John the Evangelist, asserting

Michelet remarks that to derive *assassin* from *hashishin* is like deriving *cheval* from *equus*, and he seems to find the use of hashish unworthy of Hassan-ibn-Sabbah. The etymology that I give here is abundantly confirmed by Sylvestre de Sacy, von Hammer, and several other historians. Moreover, many secret societies, Persian, Indian and Chinese, have made and still make use of beverages based on hashish, opium and many other plants, in order to promote the emergence of the astral "double" and the attainment of the early degrees of ecstasy.

that he was the founder of the true church. The Roman Church was not the lawful Church, and the missionaries of Peter, when they preached among the heathen, had debased the conceptions of Jesus. According to the Johannites it was blasphemy to say that Jesus had mounted the cross, for the son of God could not have been crucified. After John, the Johannite patriarchs had succeeded one another without interruption. The last of them was Theocletes, who was wandering obscurely about Palestine. If, however, he could find supporters his Church would triumph over false Churches, and his successor would be the most powerful man in Christendom.

Hugues des Payens gathered round him seven knights and founded an order of chivalry whose ostensible aim was to protect pilgrims journeying to the Holy Land. He called it the Order of the Temple, because its mystic and secret aim was the reconstitution of the Temple of Solomon, the symbol of perfection. This symbol had been confined in the geometry of the stones; it was the pursuit of divine wisdom and its realisation under the hierarchical direction of initiates. Material power was to be the means of raising the Temple.

This material power was acquired with a speed which surpassed all the dreams of the founders.

In 1128 Hugues des Payens came to France and had the rule of the new Order approved by St Bernard. It was ascetic and warlike. If it strangely resembled the rules of the secret societies of the East, nobody was aware of the fact. The Templars were divided into three grades: knights, men-at-arms and affiliates. They obeyed the Grand Master, but there was an inner order composed of seven members, who remained unknown and who carried on the original tradition.

Their uniform was a white robe with a red cross on the left side. They were exempted from taxes and from military service to kings. They might be tried only by the pope. The number three played a particular part in their ritual. When a candidate wished to be admitted knight he knocked thrice on the door of the church in which the ceremony was to be performed, and he was thrice asked what he wanted. Every knight had to have three horses, keep three great fasts and communicate three times a year. Those who had committed a fault were scourged thrice. They took three vows.

After the lapse of a few years they had accumulated enormous riches and constituted an ever-increasing force among the nations of Europe and in the East. Their strength came from their financial operations.

During the hundred and eighty-four years of the existence of the Order the aim was never lost sight of and was pursued with stubborn determination. They had their castles in every country, numbering about nine thousand. They made uninterrupted progress. When they fought the Egyptians, the Syrians and the Order of Assassins, they learned their enemies' customs, military organisation and doctrine. When they built their fortresses, it was on the plan of the Saracen fortresses, and they can thus be easily distinguished from those of the Hospitallers, their rivals.

Close relations, in the form of alliances concluded and then broken, often united the Templars with the Saracens. They betrayed Frederick II for the Sultan of Babylon. On another occasion they refused to fight the infidels in support of Leon, King of Armenia. After the capture of Damietta, Imbert, Marshal of the Temple and confidant of the papal legate, Cardinal Pelagius, who was in command of the Christian army, suddenly left that army, which was stuck fast in the overflow of the Nile, and went over to the Mussulmans. If it is a true story that it was a Knight Templar who prevented the Grand Master of the Assassins from becoming converted to Christianity and killed his ambassador, it was no doubt because he did not believe in so improbable a conversion and saw in it nothing but a ruse of war.

All this proves the closeness of the affinity between the Knights Templar and their enemies. They neither hesitated to betray Christendom when it was to their interest, nor, when they took Mussulman prisoners, did they allow them to go without ransom. The fact was that for them the only truth lay in the increase of their power.

With the years the Grand Masters became more powerful, and power brought with it only increased ambition. Under Thomas Berard they fought the Hospitallers with at least as great enthusiasm as if they had been fighting the infidels. But human life did not count in their eyes. A great concrete plan can be carried out only by means of the indiscriminate killing of friend and enemy alike. Nothing counted to them, neither the authority of the pope, which they threw off more and more every day, nor moral laws, nor the laws of chivalry. We will give only one significant example.

The Christians had almost everywhere been expelled from the East, where for nearly three centuries they had destroyed the monuments of Arab art, burned libraries* and created around them a desolation which can only be compared to that caused by the Mongols.† Sultan Khalil had laid siege to Acre, whose defence had been entrusted to the Grand Master of the Temple, Guillaume de Beaujeu. He was killed on the ramparts when the contest had lasted several months, and since the besieged town contained the number of priors necessary for an election, his successor was at once proclaimed, the monk Gaudini. The new Grand Master was an intellectual and a philosopher rather than a soldier. He at once tried to negotiate terms of surrender, but he was too late, and the town was pillaged. The wives and daughters of the nobles of the town had taken refuge in the fortress of the Templars, which overlooked the sea and allowed resistance to be continued. Nightfall interrupted fighting and pillage. The Knights Templar were called upon to surrender and agreed to do so provided they were allowed to withdraw on the following day with the women who had taken refuge behind their walls. The Sultan accepted this condition, but it was agreed that a few hundred Mussulman soldiers should occupy one of the towers in order to ensure that the conditions of surrender were adhered to. Unfortunately this tower was that

* Notably the library of Tripoli, which contained more than 100,000 volumes.

† I find it difficult to understand the admiration that history text-books profess for what they call " the great mystical movements of the Crusades." Behind the chivalry of France the scum of the West rushed to pillage the East. St Bernard fairly described these Crusaders, whose enthusiasm he had aroused : " That which is pleasing about this mob, this torrent rushing to the Holy Land, is the fact that it consists of nothing but scoundrels and ungodly men. But Christ has transformed his enemies into his champions."

in which the women were crowded. The Mussulman soldiers, drunk with success, could not control themselves at the sight of the women. They dragged them off into the church of the Order and violated them. The knights heard the screams and rushed off to inform the Grand Master of the treachery and consult him as to the vengeance to be exacted.

Gaudini shrugged his shoulders and replied :

" I am no less distressed than you, gentlemen. But what can we do in such circumstances ? "*

And he hurriedly embarked with the Temple archives and a dozen of the higher officers of the Order in a ship which escaped under cover of darkness and reached Cyprus. The rape of three hundred women was of no importance provided the few men who had in hand the conquest and organisation of Europe were saved.

The Templars who remained behind killed the Sultan's soldiers, but on the following day they perished together with the Christian women ; the tower in which they were defending themselves fell at the moment of assault, burying in its ruins conquerors and conquered.

Some years later, during the Grand Mastership of Jacques de Molay, all the proud towers of the Temple which had been built at the cross-roads of Europe collapsed simultaneously.

* Père Mansuet, *Histoire critique de l'Ordre des Chevaliers du Temple.*

THE DENIAL OF JESUS AND OTHER CHARGES AGAINST THE TEMPLARS

IT was the period when Philippe le Bel had just debased the coinage of France for his own benefit. In spite of the debasement he still remained without money. One day he received a letter from the governor of a château in Languedoc, near Béziers. The governor informed him that a citizen of that town, named Squint de Florian, who had been condemned to death, asked to be allowed to speak to the king before his execution, saying that he had a secret of unprecedented importance to reveal to him. The governor had had the execution deferred.

Impelled by curiosity the king had Florian sent to Paris. Florian threw himself at the king's feet and begged his life in exchange for a secret. His petition was granted. This is what he revealed.

Florian had spent some days in prison in the company of a Templar apostate, condemned to death like himself. This Templar, on the point of execution and unable to get a priest, had confessed to his companion. He confessed that before he became a criminal and while he was a member of the Order of the Temple, he had committed crimes far greater than those for which he was now to suffer death. These crimes were also committed by the flower of the chivalry of France. The Templars denied Jesus Christ and spat thrice on the Cross when they were received into the Order. They practised unnatural vice, not occasionally but with official permission and as a praiseworthy and commendable action. Finally, they dedicated themselves, by the magical rite of a cord girt round their loins, to a strange, bearded idol called Baphomet.

It is difficult to believe that Philippe le Bel, who had so little respect for the pope that he had recently boxed his ears through the agency of Nogaret, was shocked by the heresy or the worship of Baphomet, or by the practice of sodomy, which was common at that time. It is probable that there was revealed to him something of the Templars' ambitious ideal of conquest. This ideal, known only to the inner group of Grand Priors, must have percolated through and been whispered abroad as a doubtful legend; it had not sufficient body to be included in the accusations at the trial. But knowledge of it must have made Philippe le Bel reflect upon the extraordinary power which had arisen within his kingdom but outside his authority. He must suddenly have grasped the possible imminence of a great danger and realised that if he swiftly removed the danger by an audacious stroke he could at the same time enrich himself by confiscating the immense wealth of the Order of the Temple. His fear, which rested on nothing but the vaguest evidence and was never formally confirmed, is the only justification of the greatest crime, after the massacre of the Albigenses, that a pope and a King of France ever committed jointly.

Perhaps the time had come for the great realisation of the plans of the Order. The Mussulmans had expelled the Christians from Palestine and Egypt. How was it possible to utilise the tremendous energy of these soldiers, to whom fighting was a vital necessity? Almost all the revenues of the Order had been devoted to the upkeep of their fortresses and possessions in the East. With the cessation of the war against the infidels enormous sums would be set free. A Templar named Roger de Flor considered that the moment had come. He had just been expelled from the Order for stealing part of its treasure at the fall of Acre and for ill-treating some Christian women who had taken refuge on his galley. Alone, at the head of some Spanish adventurers, he tried to found a Mediterranean kingdom. He escaped the pursuit of the pope and of the Order, won a huge fortune and obtained from the Emperor of Constantinople the hand of his niece Marie and the title of Cæsar.

The Grand Master, Jacques de Molay, had not the decisiveness he needed. Everyone liked him. Honesty and average qualities predominated in him. These do not lead a man far. A single fact seems to make it probable that the Temple judged the time ripe to carry out their great scheme in Europe. When the pope, acting in conjunction with Philippe le Bel, summoned Jacques de Molay to Poitiers, he recommended him to come incognito and almost unaccompanied. But Jacques de Molay left Cyprus, where he then was, with a great retinue, the flower of the knights and the Temple treasure. That might well have been an indication that he regarded the field of action of the Order as being thenceforward in Europe, where he would need all his fighting men.

Cleverly and hypocritically the King lavished on Jacques de Molay and the Templars every mark of friendship and favour, while Clement V, for his part, could refuse the king nothing. He had been elected pope thanks to the King of France. Public opinion was worked up, and for the first time the university and the people were to be asked to approve a royal decision. But the very character of the charges would give popularity to a sudden stroke of this kind. For a long time there had been rumours as to the disappearance and mysterious death of men who had been imprudent enough to be present at a secret ceremony of the Temple.

The Templars were everywhere hated. "It was said that they were notoriously in relations with the Assassins of Syria. The people observed with fear the likeness between their uniform and that of the followers of the Old Man of the Mountain. They had received the Sultan in their houses, had permitted Mohammedan worship. In their furious rivalry with the Hospitallers they had gone so far as to shoot their arrows against the Holy Sepulchre."*

It was considered scandalous that the court of the Grand Master should be more numerous and more magnificent than the court of kings. Exception was taken to the occult character of initiation into the Order. Men spoke in whispers of magic, of the ritual murder of children. Philippe le Bel would find allies in the anger and hatred which a people feels for all that it does not understand.

During the night of the 13th of October, 1306, Jacques de Molay was arrested, together with all the knights who were in Paris. Orders had been sent in advance to the provinces that all the Templars in France were to be arrested simultaneously. Torture produced more

* Michelet, *Histoire de France*.

than a hundred and forty confessions. But when the house of the Temple was searched, neither the archives of the Order, nor the original authentic rule, nor the rite of initiation was found. Jacques de Molay, impressed by rumours that had been current some days before with regard to a danger threatening the Order, had had them removed and hidden in a safe place. They have never been found.

The Templars were accused of denying Jesus Christ and of spitting thrice on the Cross when they took their vows of fidelity. This charge has been endlessly discussed and various explanations of it suggested. That which has been adopted by many men of sound judgment, notably by Michelet,* is that this form of initiation was borrowed from the ancient mysteries. In order to bring into greater relief the perfect purity of the initiate after initiation, he had to appear before initiation as having attained the last degree of irreligion. He denied Jesus. The deeper his fall had been the more thoroughly he was rehabilitated by entry into the Order. At the time of the trial of the Templars the rite was practised, though its symbolical meaning had been lost.

This explanation is rather childish ; but how can an action which must have seemed monstrous to Christians have been demanded of them without the reason for it being given, when the reason was so simple ? The question must constantly have been asked ; for a pious knight, invited, on admission into the Order, to spit on that which he had been taught to worship, must have undergone tortures. It would have been easy to soothe

* In spite of the explanation he gives, Michelet is horrified at the grossness of the profanation.

his conscience, and an answer so readily understood would soon have been forgotten!

Actually, the numerous knights who either begged their initiator to excuse them the ceremony of denial of the Cross or hoped to evade its consequences by a mental reservation, could not be given the true explanation without at the same time knowing the secrets of the Order. And these secrets were kept for a deeper initiation, entry into the inner group.

The act of spitting on the Cross signified the Templar's liberation from the Roman Church, which thenceforward he would no longer serve in heart. Just as the Assassins, who were the enemies of official Islam, enjoined on their disciples of the early grades rigorous observance of the Koran, so the Order of the Temple taught a Christianity which was rigorous in form. But in the spirit the bond which joined each member of the Order to the Church was broken by the ceremony of initiation. He was bound to a higher Church, to a Christ who could not die on the Cross; and a day would come when he would have to fight the Pope of Rome and his bishops, and then he would need to remember his initiation as a living act.

The Templars were, in fact, so far detached from the Catholic Church that they did not use consecrated wafers at mass, and received confession from their visitors and preceptors, who often were laymen.

The charge of unnatural vice weighed as heavily on them as that of heresy. Not that sodomy during the middle ages was not very widespread. On the contrary, it seems to have been more so than in ancient Greece, more so even than in the great cities of our times. "In the eighth century, according to Alcuin, and probably in the succeeding centuries, every bishop was obliged, upon election and before consecration, to vindicate himself in respect of the following canonical questions: (1) If he had been a pederast; (2) If he had had criminal commerce with a nun; (3) If he had had criminal commerce with 'a four-footed beast'."* And he was compelled to swear that he would never subsequently practise any form of criminal commerce. The fact that an episcopal candidate should have been so persistently interrogated with regard to such acts means that they must have been common. But, as in our own day, anything was tolerated or even permitted, provided it was done secretly, provided hypocrisy enveloped it with its ashen cloak.

Many witnesses deposed that when they entered the Order they were recommended by their superior to practise sodomy amongst themselves and to abstain from the love of women. This revelation aroused great anger throughout the world, but the anger was not entirely justified. Complete chastity was put forward as an ideal, which, however, could not be immediately realised. Sodomy was a first step towards it, a fining down of sensual exaltation. Moreover the Templars were, before anything else, warriors, who took castles and towns. The custom in those days was to rape the women of a town that had been captured. Those who resisted, and sometimes those who had been raped and discarded, were killed. So widely established was this custom that in the twelfth century a special order of chivalry was

* Frédéric Nicolai. *Essai sur les accusations intentées aux Templiers et sur le secret de cet ordre.*

founded to protect women during the march of armies and after the capture of towns. It was possibly with an idea of humane economy that a wise Grand Master recommended sodomy as a makeshift.

In the history of mystical sects there are analogous examples. Those who find material life irretrievably bad are only logical in refusing to perpetuate it. In this event they find an outlet for their senses by an act which brings a minimum of pleasure and has no consequences. Proceedings, which attracted a good deal of attention at the time, were taken in India some thirty years ago against a philosopher whose teachings were of this nature. Actually, all misunderstandings arise from the inordinate importance which religions and societies attach to men's physical relations. These relations, the interest of which varies with the age and intelligence of each individual, ought to possess importance only in so far as they develop a feeling for beauty, and love in the highest sense of the word.

But a rule such as that of the Order of the Temple did not allow for the baseness of instincts, or for the total absence of even the rudiments of spirituality in the great majority of men. And most Templars saw in it nothing more than licence for a pleasure which till then was regarded as forbidden. All the rites of the Order were debased.

The kiss on the lips given to a candidate at his reception into the Order, which was the communication of breath, of force, in accordance with the practice of secret societies in the East, became a symbol of pleasure. But the reception of the knight was very often the pretext for ludicrous and indecent scenes, in which defenders of the Temple and lovers of symbols cannot possibly discover a hidden meaning. During the examination at Cahors a knight named Arnaud deposed that immediately after his reception, " at which he had given and received criminal kisses, the superior who received him had at once misused him."*

At Carcassonne a young knight named Jean de Cassagne confessed that " while a priest of the Order was reading a psalm the superior kissed him on the mouth, lay on the bench on which he was sitting, that they exchanged other kisses, and that the ten knights kissed him on the navel. Then the superior took out of a box a copper idol. . . ."

The third charge was connected with this idol. It was named *Baphomet.*† The one which was found in Paris was numbered, for each chapter of the Temple possessed one. It was made of copper and had a long white beard. It has been variously described, for the knight saw it when he was initiated only for a few seconds. It has been said that it was a kind of marionette, that it had the face of a cat, and that it represented Satan. These puerilities helped to give some foundation to the suspicion

* *Histoire de l'abolition de l'Ordre des Templiers*, 1779.

† There are three possible derivations of this word :

(1) According to the oldest and possibly the commonest explanation, it is a corruption of the word *Mahomet*. It was a frequent charge against the Templars that they inclined to Mohammedanism.

(2) Von Hammer's explanation is that the word is a combination of the two Greek words βαφή (baptism) and μῆτις (wisdom), the Gnostic baptism.

(3) Eliphas Lévi in his *Dogme et rituel de la haute magie* says that the word was formed cabalistically by writing in reverse order the initial letters of the Latin words, templi omnium hominum pacis abbas (abbot [or father] of the temple of peace of all men). Thus : TEM O H P AB.—*Trans.*

of heresy which hung over the Temple. The knights were convinced that they were worshipping an Oriental deity.

In reality, Baphomet was a symbol of Gnostic origin, intended to embody the doctrine of the Temple and to recall its aim. It was neither the figure of Jupiter nor that of Mohammed that was worshipped in it; it was power that was worshipped, power directed by intelligence, which was the ideal of the Temple and which was always represented in ancient symbolism by a bearded man wearing a crown. This bearded man is found on the seals and medallions belonging to the Templars. It was for them what the rose in the middle of the cross was for the Rosicrucians, the symbol of the sublime ideal to which they had dedicated their lives. The flaxen cord given to every new knight, which he was instructed to wear under his garment, had to touch Baphomet because it symbolised the bond which links man with his ideal.

THE FALL OF THE ORDER

I SHALL not tell in detail the story of the trial of the Templars, which lasted seven years. The hoped-for confessions of heresy were quickly extorted from a great many of them by torture. The Grand Master himself was unable to withstand it. But his confessions must have been falsified by the three cardinals who heard them, for when they were read over to him he did not recognise them; he said he preferred Saracen trials "in which the prisoner's head was cut off at once."

At first Clement V seemed to hold his hand, dismayed at the grossness of the injustice. But interest bound him to the King of France. Besides, he coveted the riches of the Templars, with which he hoped to satisfy the demands of the beautiful Brunissende, Comtesse de Foix.

The striking feature of the trial was the terror inspired by the king's justice. Not a man dared raise his voice in defence of the Templars. After two years of shuffling and preliminary tortures a papal commission was solemnly installed in the palace of the Archbishop of Paris, where it sat every day to hear the defence. Every day an usher appeared on the threshold of the palace and cried out: "If any man wishes to defend the Military Order of the Temple, let him come forward." But no one came forward. Four months passed by, and on every day of them the same ceremony was repeated. At last, one day a man clothed in black made his way through the silent crowd and demanded to be heard in defence of the Order. A thrill ran through the multitudes that thronged the streets and the commissioners rose to their feet in great emotion. The man's name was Jean de Melot. He had been a Templar for ten years. He had much to say; he would prove the Order innocent. When attention was at its height, he said that he wanted food immediately, that he was a very poor man, and that he hoped someone would help him. It was seen then that he was a simple. The food that he had asked for was given him, and the possibility of hearing any defence of the Order of the Temple was dismissed.

There was never to be any defence. Apparently, every knight had lost his wits. The Grand Master asserted that he was a man of war, unable to argue logically. After two years of captivity he requested eight days for thought and permission for a chaplain to say mass for him. Had terror of torture clouded the minds of the prisoners? Had the investigation obliterated all sign of human intelligence? In any case, the mysterious part of the trial of the Templars was the incapacity of the knights to find a reasonable defence.

Finally, after seven years, Clement nominated a council to investigate the matter and give judgment. But since the members of the council insisted on hearing witnesses and making themselves thoroughly conversant with the trial, and since they seemed to cherish a desire to acquit the Order, Clement, on his own authority, declared the council suspect of heresy and dissolved it.

A great many knights were confined in the royal

prisons. By the orders of Philippe le Bel all of them who had retracted their original confessions were hurriedly condemned to death by a tribunal presided over by the Archbishop of Sens (the brother of the king's minister Marigny), on whose ferocity Philippe could safely rely.

"Near the abbey of Saint-Antoine fifteen or twenty stakes had been put up and set alight. Flames did not proceed from them; they were like so many beds of coal, intended to roast the culprits by slow degrees. Fifty-four knights were thrown on to them."*

The Grand Master, Jacques de Molay, and the master of the lodge of Normandy had been condemned to perpetual imprisonment. But at the last minute, in the presence of the Archbishop of Sens, they suddenly retracted their confessions. They declared that "the Order was pure and holy and that they were ready to die to uphold this truth."

They died that very day. Philippe had them conducted to the island in the Seine which is situated between the king's gardens and the Augustins. Here two stakes had been erected. The two Templars, says the historian, "had become disfigured by their long captivity." A great crowd watched the executions. There was no thick smoke to suffocate them, so that they were slowly burned. When half Jacques de Molay's body had been consumed, tradition relates that he cried, "Clement, thou wicked judge, I summon thee to appear before the tribunal of God forty days from now. And thee, King Philippe, unjust likewise, I summon within a year."

* *Histoire de l'abolition de l'Ordre des Templiers.*

Forty days afterwards Clement died of lupus near Avignon. The King of France survived him only eight months. It is said also that a Templar of Beaucaire, on his way to the stake, met Nogaret, the king's councillor and instigator of the trial, and foretold his imminent death. Florian and the prior of Montfaucon who had followed him in denouncing the Order were both murdered within the year.

Some have seen in these coincidences a proof of certain magical powers which have been ascribed to the Templars. But no explanation has been given of why these powers were never manifested during the seven years of the trial. It may be that there is an inferior magic which can be used only for purposes of vengeance.

* * * * * *

A legend current in the south of France relates that, in the church of the little Pyrenean village of Gavarnie, there have been preserved the heads of nine executed Templars. Every year at midnight on the 13th of October, the anniversary of the fall of the Order, a voice echoes through the church: "Has the day come for the liberation of the Sepulchre of Christ?" And the nine heads flutter their mummied eyelids, and through their mummied lips whisper the reply: "Not yet!"

The liberation of the Sepulchre of Christ was originally understood symbolically as the liberation of the spirit. This legend shows that in the land of the Albigenses the aim of the Order had been understood, and even after its destruction the promised liberation was not despaired of.

The only effect of the papal bulls suppressing the

Order was to make it thenceforward secret. Jacques de Molay in his prison had nominated as his successor John Mark Larmenius, of Jerusalem, who was succeeded in his turn by Thibaut of Alexandria; since when the Order has continued its existence, and "the succession of its Grand Masters, who have included many illustrious and influential men, has never been interrupted."*

Jacques de Molay's nephew, de Beaujeu, collected his ashes and became the possessor of the archives and secrets of the Order. Followed by several knights he went to Scotland, where Edward II gave them land. This little group acknowledged as their leader the head of the Freemasons, Henry FitzEdwin, who formed the Edinburgh lodge. Others of them went to Sweden. In subsequent centuries the Templars became Freemasons and played an active part in the development of the movement. But a study of the part they played and of its influence on the French Revolution is too big a subject for me to deal with here. I will mention only the final act in the drama, which shows, if it is authentic, that the Templar connection was still actively alive in the early days of the Revolution, and that there is a direct relation of cause and effect between the death of Jacques de Molay and the death of Louis XVI.

The second after the head of Louis XVI had fallen under the guillotine, a man, who had been observed taking part in all the street demonstrations since the taking of the Bastille, rushed forward on to the scaffold, scooped up some of the royal blood in his hands, made the gesture of scattering it over the crowd and cried:

* Le Couteulx de Canteleu, *Les sectes et les sociétés secrètes.*

"People of France, I baptise you in the name of Jacques de Molay and in the name of freedom!"*

Jacques de Molay was revenged. Possibly the Order had had no other aim than this revenge for five centuries.

From that time onwards the Order is met with only in weakened form. At the beginning of the nineteenth century some of its members tried to reconstitute it, but only partially. This attempt was made with the consent of Napoleon, who meant to extract from the Order the greatest possible advantage to himself, perhaps even to become its Grand Master when the Order should have won social importance. He sent a regiment of infantry to line the road in front of the church of Saint-Paul Saint-Antoine when a memorial service was held, in 1808, to celebrate the anniversary of Jacques de Molay's death. All the new Templars took part in this ceremony, sitting enthroned in the church. They wore ermine-bordered cloaks and had pectoral crosses, epaulettes, fillets, fringed girdles and white boots with red heels. The first thing they had done, after distributing titles and dignities, was to invent these magnificent uniforms. It is, unfortunately, a characteristic of many sects who think they are seeking a truly spiritual aim, to suppose that an initiate must wear the uniform of an initiate, and that spiritual development can be signalised only by variety of symbols and selection of colours and materials. The search for this easy superiority can be found in academies, in philharmonic and other societies, and in other groupings in which human vanity finds expression.

The new Order of the Temple was modified a little

* This story is told by Eliphas Lévi and reproduced by Stanislas de Guaita.

later under the direction of Fabré Palaprat, a doctor, who tried to restore the Johannite religion. Here he was in the genuine Templar tradition of Theocletes and Hugues des Payens. He based his beliefs on a mysterious manuscript called the Leviticon, which he said he had found and which, according to him, contained the secret doctrines of the Templars of the thirteenth century. But nothing came of his attempt, except a distribution of new dignities and new uniforms.

The Order of the Temple has now disappeared, and its disappearance marks the complete defeat of its great designs. The church of John has lost its heroic champions. The liberation of the spirit and the organisation of the world by a group of initiates who have knowledge, has not been and will not be realised, as the nine heads witness, under the brick and slate of Gavarnie. The wearers of the white cloak with the red cross over the heart, who might have attempted these aims, died in the prisons of Philippe le Bel, after being disgraced by the investigations of the Dominican Inquisitors.

But the spirit could not be liberated by the Templars. A great design cannot be carried out by that which is based on a hypocrisy. The Order of the Temple taught its knights to practise the strictest Catholicism, just as the Order of the Assassins based its teachings on the rules of the Koran. But both Orders wished to destroy the Church which they outwardly venerated, in order to found a more perfect Church on the ruins. Hulagu's Mongol cavalry and the far-seeing prudence of Philippe le Bel made an end of these great powers of the East and West.

If the Templars had triumphed, history would have

been altered in a way that we cannot now foresee. They had understood the necessity for the union of religions. Their close relationship with Islam and its philosophers had taught them to respect the civilisation of their enemies, and even to adopt it. Their social plans included the rise of the third estate. Who knows what the nations of Europe might have become in the hands of this aristocratic army. Would they have been transformed by the factor of spiritual progress? Or —and this is the more likely—would they have bowed under the iron tyranny invariably wielded by the possessors of physical force?

The original recipients of the message had been certain knight-mystics of the first Crusade, who wished to hand it on by the sword. But the great truths that they had learned at Jerusalem were incomplete. They did not know that the Word loses its virtue with the reek of the blood that is shed for it. There is a certain spiritual light which dies upon contact with the metal of armour, with the steel of the sword. And if he who wishes to hand it on is enveloped with the magnetism of gold, the light becomes darkness. If certain truths are to keep their original purity they need to be spoken by the lips of poor men; the gesture that introduces them must be made by a hand whitened by asceticism and long prayer.

Whether the charges brought against the Templars were true or false, whether initiations degenerated into the orgies found among so many mystical sects, is a question of little importance. Nor does it matter that the eyes of Baphomet were brilliant carbuncles, or that the denial of Christ took such and such a form. Their real crime was never mentioned at the trial. How should it have been? It was committed daily by Philippe le Bel and Clement V.

Having lost their first ideal, the Templars had taken the means for the end. These destroying monks became greedy bankers, acquirers of fortresses and towns, money-lenders, lords of vassals and feudal lands. Why did they not keep the divine light-heartedness of the days of their youth, when they rushed along the shores of Lake Tiberias in defence of the pilgrims! They were so poor at that time that two of them shared one horse. Those were the days when they held Jerusalem for the Christians. When each of them had several finely-caparisoned horses they were driven out of Acre. The secret of their power lay in their courage and faith. But they took wealth for their ideal, as the Albigenses had taken poverty. They laid claim to a Christ higher than the Christ worshipped by the common herd; but they had not so much as heard of the parable of the camel and the eye of a needle. They believed that in order to carry out a great work they might with impunity make use of the weapons of evil.

And so their message was lost, their work wiped out, like all work the first principle of which is not perfect disinterestedness.

NICOLAS FLAMEL AND THE PHILOSOPHER'S STONE

THE BOOK OF ABRAHAM THE JEW

WISDOM has various means for making its way into the heart of man. Sometimes a prophet comes forward and speaks. Or a sect of mystics receives the teaching of a philosophy, like rain on a summer evening, gathers it in and spreads it abroad with love. Or it may happen that a charlatan, performing tricks to astonish men, may produce, perhaps without knowing it himself, a ray of real light with his dice and magic mirrors. In the fourteenth century the pure truth of the masters was transmitted by a book. This book fell into the hands of precisely the man who was destined to receive it; and he, with the help of the text and the hieroglyphic diagrams which taught the transmutation of metals into gold, accomplished the transmutation of his soul, which is a far rarer and more wonderful operation.

Thanks to the amazing book of Abraham the Jew all the hermetists of the following centuries had the opportunity of admiring an example of a perfect life, that of Nicolas Flamel, the man who received the book. After his death or disappearance many students and alchemists who had devoted their lives to the search for the philosopher's stone despaired because they had not in their possession the wonderful book in which was contained the secret of gold and of eternal life. But their despair was unnecessary. The secret had become alive. The magic formulæ had become incarnate in the actions of a man. No ingot of virgin gold melted in the crucibles could, in colour or purity, attain the beauty of the wise bookseller's pious life.

There is nothing legendary about the life of Nicolas Flamel. The Bibliothèque Nationale contains works copied in his hand and original works written by him. All the official documents relating to his life have been found, his marriage contract, his deeds of gift, his will. His history rests solidly on those substantial material proofs for which men clamour if they are to believe in the most obvious things (whenever those obvious things are also beautiful). To this indisputably authentic history legend has added a few flowers. But in every spot where the flowers of legend grow, underneath there is the solid earth of truth.

Whether Nicolas Flamel was born at Pontoise or somewhere else, a question which historians have investigated with extreme attention, seems to me to be entirely without importance. It is enough to know that towards the middle of the fourteenth century he was carrying on the trade of a bookseller and had a stall backing on to the columns of Saint-Jacques la Boucherie.

It was not a big stall, for it measured only two feet by two and a half. However, it grew. He bought a house in the old rue de Marivaux and used the ground-floor for his business. Copyists and illuminators did their work there. He himself gave a few writing lessons and taught nobles who could only sign their names with a cross. One of the copyists or illuminators acted also as a servant to him.

Nicolas Flamel married Pernelle, a good-looking,

intelligent widow, slightly older than himself and the possessor of a little property.

Every man meets once in his life the woman with whom he could live in peace and harmony. For Nicolas Flamel, Pernelle was that woman. Over and above her natural qualities she had another which is still rarer. She was the only woman in the history of humanity who was capable of keeping a secret all her life without revealing it to everybody in confidence.

The story of Nicolas Flamel is the story of a book. The secret made its appearance with the book. Neither the death of its possessors nor the lapse of centuries led to the complete discovery of the secret.

Nicolas Flamel had acquired some knowledge of the hermetic art. The ancient alchemy of the Egyptians and the Greeks which flourished among the Arabs had, thanks to them, penetrated to Christian countries. Nicolas Flamel did not, of course, regard alchemy as a mere vulgar search for the means of making gold. For every exalted mind the finding of the philosopher's stone was the finding of the essential secret of Nature, the secret of her unity and her laws, the possession of perfect wisdom. Flamel dreamed of sharing in this wisdom. His ideal was the highest that man can attain. And he knew that it could be realised through a book. For the secret of the philosopher's stone had already been found and transcribed in symbolic form. Somewhere it existed. It was in the hands of unknown sages who lived somewhere unknown. But how difficult it was for a small Paris bookseller to get into touch with those sages.

Nothing, then, has changed since the fourteenth

century. In our day also many men strive desperately towards an ideal, the path which they know but cannot climb; and they hope to win the magic formula (which will make them new beings) from some miraculous visit or from a book written expressly for them. But the visitor does not come and the book is not written.

But for Nicolas Flamel the book *was* written. Perhaps because a bookseller is better situated than other people to receive a unique book; perhaps because the strength of his desire organised events without his knowledge, so that the book came when it was time.

So strong was his desire, that the coming of the book was preceded by a dream, which shows that this wise and well-balanced bookseller had a tendency to mysticism.

Nicolas Flamel dreamed one night that an angel stood before him. The angel, who was radiant and winged like all angels, held a book in his hands and uttered these words, which were to remain in the memory of the hearer:

"Look well at this book. At first you will understand nothing in it, neither you nor any other man. But one day you will see in it that which no other man will be able to see."

Flamel stretched out his hand to receive the present from the angel, and the whole scene disappeared in the golden light of dreams.

Some time after that the dream was partly realised.

One day, when Nicolas Flamel was alone in his shop, an unknown man in need of money appeared with a manuscript to sell. Flamel was no doubt tempted to receive him with disdainful arrogance, as do the booksellers of our day when some poor student offers to sell them part of his library. But the moment he saw the book he recognised it as the book which the angel had held out to him, and he paid two florins for it without bargaining.

The book appeared to him indeed resplendent and instinct with divine virtue. It had a very old binding of worked copper, on which were engraved curious diagrams and certain characters, some of which were Greek and others in a language he could not decipher. The leaves of the book were not made of parchment, like those he was accustomed to copy and bind. They were made of the bark of young trees and were covered with very clear writing done with an iron point. These leaves were divided into groups of seven and consisted of three parts separated by a page without writing, but containing a diagram which was quite unintelligible to Flamel. On the first page were written words to the effect that the author of the manuscript was Abraham the Jew, prince, priest, Levite, astrologer and philosopher. Then followed great curses and threats against anyone who set eyes on it unless he was either a priest or a scribe. The word *maranatha*, which was many times repeated on every page, intensified the awe-inspiring character of the text and diagrams. But most impressive of all was the patined gold of the edges of the book, and the atmosphere of hallowed antiquity that there was about it.

Maranatha! Yet Nicolas Flamel considered that being a scribe he might read the book without fear. He felt that the secret of life and of death, the secret of the unity of Nature, the secret of the duty of the wise man, had been concealed behind the symbol of the diagrams and formulæ in the text by an initiate long since dead. He was aware that it is a rigid law for initiates that they must not reveal their knowledge, because if it is good and fruitful for the intelligent, it is bad for ordinary men. As Jesus has clearly expressed it, pearls must not be given as food to swine.

He had the pearl in his hands. It was for him to rise in the scale of man in order to be worthy to understand its purity. He must have had in his heart a hymn of thanksgiving to Abraham the Jew, whose name was unknown to him, but who had thought and laboured in past centuries and whose wisdom he was now inheriting. He must have pictured him a bald old man with a hooked nose, wearing the wretched robe of his race and writing in some dark ghetto, in order that the light of his thought might not be lost. And he must have vowed to solve the riddle, to re-kindle the light, to be patient and faithful, like the Jew who had died in the flesh but lived eternally in his manuscript.

Nicolas Flamel had studied the art of transmutation. He was in touch with all the learned men of his day. Manuscripts dealing with chemistry have been found, notably that of Almasatus, which were part of his personal library. He had knowledge of the symbols of which the alchemists made habitual use. But those which he saw in the book of Abraham the Jew remained dumb for him. In vain he copied some of the mysterious pages and set them out in his shop, in the hope that some visitor conversant with the Cabala would help him to solve the problem. He met with nothing but the laughter of sceptics and the ignorance of pseudo-scholars

—just as he would to-day if he showed the book of Abraham the Jew either to pretentious occultists or to the Académie des Inscriptions et Belles Lettres.

For twenty-one years he pondered the hidden meaning of the book. That is not long. He is favoured among men for whom twenty-one years are enough to enable him to find the key of life.

NICOLAS FLAMEL'S JOURNEY

AT the end of twenty-one years Nicolas Flamel had developed in himself sufficient wisdom and strength to hold out against the storm of light involved by the coming of truth to the heart of man. Only then did events group themselves harmoniously according to his will and allow him to realise his desire. For everything good and great that happens to a man is the result of the co-ordination of his own voluntary effort and a malleable fate.

No one in Paris could help Nicolas Flamel to understand the book. Now this book had been written by a Jew, and part of its text was in ancient Hebrew. The Jews had recently been driven out of France by persecution. Nicolas Flamel knew that many of these Jews had migrated to Spain. In towns such as Malaga and Granada, which were still under the enlightened dominion of the Arabs, there lived prosperous communities of Jews and flourishing synagogues, in which scholars and doctors were bred. Many Jews from the Christian towns of Spain took advantage of the tolerance extended by the Moorish kings and went to Granada to learn. There they copied Plato and Aristotle and returned home to spread abroad the knowledge of the ancients and of the Arab masters.

Nicolas Flamel thought that in Spain he might meet some erudite Cabalist who would translate the book of

Abraham for him. Travelling was difficult, and without a strong armed escort it was possible only for a pilgrim. Flamel alleged therefore a vow to St James of Compostela, the patron saint of his parish. This was also a means of concealing from his neighbours and friends the real purpose of his journey. The wise and faithful Pernelle was the only person who was aware of his real plans. He put on the pilgrim's attire and shell-adorned hat, took the staff, which ensured a certain measure of safety to a traveller in Christian countries, and started off for Galicia.

Since he was a prudent man and did not wish to expose the precious manuscript to the risks of travel, he contented himself with taking with him a few carefully copied pages, which he hid in his modest baggage.

Nicolas Flamel has not recounted the adventures that befell him on his journey. Possibly he had none—it may be that adventures happen only to those who want to have them. He has told us merely that he went first to fulfil his vow to St James. Then he wandered about Spain, trying to get into relations with learned Jews. But they were suspicious of Christians, particularly of the French, who had expelled them from their country. Besides, he had not much time. He had to remember Pernelle waiting for him, and his shop, which was being managed only by his servants. To a man of over fifty on his first distant journey the silent voice of his home makes a powerful appeal every evening.

In discouragement he started his homeward journey. His way lay through Leôn, where he stopped for the night at an inn and happened to sup at the same table as a French merchant from Boulogne who was travelling on business. This merchant inspired him with confidence and he whispered a few words to him of his wish to find a learned Jew. By a lucky chance the French merchant was in relations with a certain Maestro Canches, an old man who lived at Leôn, immersed in his books. Nothing was easier than to introduce this Maestro Canches to Nicolas Flamel, who decided to make one more attempt before leaving Spain.

I can picture the beauty of the scene when the profane merchant of Boulogne has left them, and the two men are face to face. The gates of the ghetto close. Maestro Canches' only thought is by a few polite words to rid himself as quickly as he can of this French bookseller, who has deliberately dulled the light in his eye and clothed himself in mediocrity; for the prudent traveller passes unnoticed. Flamel speaks, reticently at first. He admires the knowledge of the Jews. Thanks to his trade he has read a great many books. At last he timidly lets fall a name, which hitherto has aroused not a spark of interest in anyone to whom he has spoken—the name of Abraham the Jew, prince, priest, Levite, astrologer and philosopher. Suddenly Flamel sees the eyes of the feeble old man before him light up. Maestro Canches has heard of Abraham the Jew. He was a great master of the wandering race, perhaps the most venerable of all the sages who studied the mysteries of the Cabala, a higher initiate, one of those who rise the higher the better they succeed in remaining unknown. His book existed and disappeared centuries ago, but tradition says it has never been destroyed, that it is passed from hand to hand and that it always reaches the man whose destiny it is to receive it. Maestro Canches has dreamed all his life long of finding it. He is very old, close to death, and now the hope which he has almost given up is near realisation. The night goes by, and there is a light round the two heads bent over their work. Maestro Canches is translating Hebrew of the time of Moses. He is explaining symbols which originated in Chaldæa. How the years fall from these two men, inspired by their belief in truth !

But the few pages that Flamel had brought were not enough to allow the secret to be revealed. Maestro Canches made up his mind at once to accompany Flamel to Paris. His extreme old age was an obstacle. That he would defy. Jews were not allowed in France. He would be converted. For many years he had been above all religions. The two men, united by an indissoluble bond, started off along the Spanish roads.

The ways of nature are mysterious. The nearer Maestro Canches came to the realisation of his dream, the more precarious became his health ; and the breath of life weakened in him. O God ! he prayed, grant me the days I need, and that I may cross the threshold of death only when I possess the liberating secret by which darkness becomes light and flesh spirit !

But the prayer was not heard. The inflexible law had appointed the hour of the old man's death. He fell ill at Orleans and in spite of all Flamel's care died seven days later. As he had been converted and Flamel did not wish to be suspected of having brought a Jew into France, he had him piously buried in the church of Sainte-Croix and had masses said for him ; for he rightly thought that a soul which had striven for so pure an aim and had passed at the moment of fruition could not rest in the realm of disembodied spirits.

Flamel continued his journey and reached Paris, where he found Pernelle, his shop, his copyists, his manuscripts. He laid aside his pilgrim's staff. But now everything was changed. It was with a joyous heart that he went his daily journey from house to shop, that he gave writing lessons to illiterates and discussed hermetic science with the educated. From natural prudence he continued to feign ignorance, in which he succeeded all the more easily because knowledge was within him. What Maestro Canches had already taught him in deciphering a few pages of the book of Abraham the Jew was sufficient to allow of his understanding the whole book. He spent three years more in searching and in completing his knowledge, but at the end of this period the transmutation was accomplished. Having learned what materials it was necessary to put together beforehand, he followed strictly the method of Abraham the Jew and changed a half-pound of mercury first into silver, and then into virgin gold. And he accomplished the same transmutation in his soul. From his passions, mixed in an invisible crucible, the substance of the eternal spirit emerged.

THE PHILOSOPHER'S STONE

FROM this point the little bookseller became rich. He bought houses, endowed churches. But he did not use his riches to increase his personal comfort or to satisfy his vanity. He altered nothing in his modest life. With Pernelle, who had helped him in his search for the philosopher's stone, he devoted his life to helping his fellow-men. "Husband and wife lavished succour on the poor, founded hospitals, built or repaired cemeteries, restored the front of Sainte-Geneviève des Ardents and endowed the institution of the Quinze-Vingts, the blind inmates of which, in memory of this fact, came every year to the church of Saint-Jacques la Boucherie to pray for their benefactor, a practice which continued until 1789."*

At the same time that he was learning how to make gold out of any material, he acquired the wisdom of despising it in his heart. Thanks to the book of Abraham the Jew he had risen above the satisfaction of his senses and the turmoil of his passions. He knew that man attains immortality only by the victory of spirit over matter, by essential purification, by the transmutation of the human into the divine. He devoted the last part of his life to what Christians call the working out of their salvation.

He attained his object without fasting or asceticism,

* Louis Figuier.

keeping the unimportant place that destiny had assigned him, continuing to copy manuscripts, buying and selling, in his little shop in the rue Saint-Jacques la Boucherie. For him there was no more mystery about the cemetery of the Innocents, which was near his house and under the arcades of which he liked to walk in the evenings. If he had the vaults and monuments restored at his own expense, it was nothing more than compliance with the custom of his time. He knew that the dead who had been laid to rest there were not concerned with stones and inscriptions and that they would return, when their hour came, in different forms, to perfect themselves and die anew. He knew the trifling extent to which he could help them. He had no temptation to divulge the secret which had been entrusted to him through the book, for he was able to measure the lowest degree of virtue necessary for the possession of it, and he knew that the revelation of the secret to an undeveloped soul only increased the imperfection of that soul.

And when he was illuminating a manuscript and putting in with a fine brush a touch of sky-blue into the eye of an angel, or of white into a wing, no smile played on his grave face, for he knew that pictures are useful to children; moreover, it is possible that beautiful fantasies which are pictured with love and sincerity may become realities in the dream of death.

Though he knew how to make gold, Nicolas Flamel made it only three times in the whole of his life; and then not for himself, for he never changed his way of life; he did it only to mitigate the evils which he saw around him. And this is the touchstone which allows us to recognise that he really attained the state of adept.

This touchstone can be used by everyone and at all times. To distinguish a man's superiority, there is but a single sign, a practical—and not an alleged—contempt for riches. However great may be a man's active virtues or the radiant power of his intelligence, if they are accompanied by the love of money which most eminent men possess, it is certain that they are tainted with baseness. What they create under the hypocritical pretext of good, will bear within it the seeds of decay. Unselfishness alone is creative, and it alone can help to raise man.

Flamel's generous gifts aroused curiosity and even jealousy. It seemed amazing that a poor bookseller should found almshouses and hospitals, should build houses with low rents, churches and convents. Rumours reached the ears of the king, Charles VI, who ordered Cramoisi, a member of the Council of State, to investigate the matter. But thanks to Flamel's prudence and reticence the result of the inquiries was favourable to him.

The rest of Flamel's life passed without special event. It was the life of a scholar. He went from his house in the rue de Marivaux to his shop. He walked in the cemetery of the Innocents, for the imagination of death was pleasant to him. He handled beautiful parchments. He illuminated missals. He smiled on Pernelle as she grew old, and he knew that life holds few better things than the peace of daily work and a calm affection.

Pernelle died first. Nicolas Flamel reached the age of eighty. He spent the last years of his life writing books on alchemy. He carefully settled his affairs and how he was to be buried, at the end of the nave of Saint-Jacques la Boucherie. The tomb-stone to be laid over his body had already been made. On this stone, in the middle of various figures, there was carved a sun above a key and a closed book. It was the symbol of his life.* His death, to which he joyfully looked forward, was as circumspect and as perfect as his life.

As it is equally useful to study men's weaknesses as their finest qualities, we may mark Flamel's weakness. This sage, who attached importance only to the immortality of his soul and despised the ephemeral form of the body, was inspired as he grew old with a strange taste for the sculptural representation of his body and face. Whenever he had a church built, or even restored, he requested the sculptor to represent him, piously kneeling, in a corner of the pediment of the façade. He had himself twice sculptured on an arch in the cemetery of the Innocents, once as he was in his youth, and once old and infirm. When he had a new house built (called "the house with the big gable") in the rue de Montmorency, on the outskirts of Paris, eleven saints were carved on the front, but a side door was surmounted with a bust of Flamel.

It seems, then, that however great a man's wisdom, however far he carries his desire to break away from his physical form, he cannot prevent himself cherishing a secret affection for that unbeautiful form, and insists that the memory of what he proclaimed contemptible should nevertheless be perpetuated in stone.

* Flamel's tomb-stone is in the Musée de Cluny, in Paris.

HISTORY OF THE BOOK OF ABRAHAM THE JEW

THE bones of sages seldom rest in peace in their grave. Perhaps Nicolas Flamel knew this and tried to protect his remains by ordering a tombstone of great weight and by having a religious service held for him twelve times a year. But these precautions were useless.

Hardly was Flamel dead when the report of his alchemical powers and of his concealment somewhere of an enormous quantity of gold spread through Paris and the world. Everyone who was seeking the famous projection powder, which turns all substances into gold, came prowling round all the places where he had lived in the hope of finding a minute portion of the precious powder. It was said also that the symbolical figures which he had had sculptured on various monuments gave, for those who could decipher it, the formula of the philosopher's stone. There was not a single alchemist but came in pilgrimage to study the sacred science on the stones of Saint-Jacques la Boucherie or the cemetery of the Innocents. The sculptures and inscriptions were broken off at night and removed. The cellars of his house were searched and the walls examined. "Towards the middle of the sixteenth century a man who had a well-known name and good credentials, which were no doubt fictitious, presented himself before the parish board of Saint-Jacques la Boucherie. He said he wished to carry out the vow of a dead friend, a pious alchemist, who, on his death-bed, had given him a sum of money with which to repair Flamel's house. The board accepted the offer. The unknown man had the cellars ransacked under the pretext of strengthening the foundations; wherever he saw a hieroglyph he found some reason for knocking down the wall at that point. Undeceived at last, he disappeared, forgetting to pay the workmen."*

A Capuchin friar and a German baron are said to have discovered in the house some stone phials full of a reddish powder, no doubt the projection powder. By the seventeenth century the various houses which had belonged to Flamel were despoiled of their ornaments and decorations, and there was nothing of them left but the four bare walls.

But what had happened to the book of Abraham the Jew? Nicolas Flamel had bequeathed his papers and library to a nephew named Perrier, who was interested in alchemy and of whom he was very fond. Absolutely nothing is known of Perrier. He no doubt benefited by his uncle's teachings and spent a sage's life in the munificent obscurity which Flamel prized so dearly, but had not been able altogether to maintain during the last years of his life. For two centuries the precious heritage was handed down from father to son, without anything being heard of it. Traces of it are found again in the reign of Louis XIII. A descendant of Flamel, named Dubois, who must still have possessed a supply of the projection powder, threw off the wise reserve of

* Albert Poisson, *Nicolas Flamel.*

his ancestors and used the powder to dazzle his contemporaries. In the presence of the king he changed leaden balls with it into gold. As a result of this experiment he had many interviews with Cardinal de Richelieu, who wished to extract his secret. Dubois, who possessed the powder but was unable to understand either Flamel's manuscripts or the book of Abraham the Jew, could tell him nothing and was imprisoned at Vincennes. It was found that he had committed certain offences in the past, and this enabled Richelieu to get him condemned to death and confiscate his property for his own benefit. At the same time the proctor of the Châtelet, no doubt by order of Richelieu, seized the houses that Flamel had owned and had them searched from top to bottom.

It was impossible to hide altogether, though the attempt was made, the profanation of the church of Saint-Jacques la Boucherie. Robbers made their way in during the night, lifted Flamel's tombstone and broke his coffin. It was after this that the rumour was first spread that the coffin had been found empty, and that it had never contained the body of Flamel, who was supposed to be still alive.

Richelieu took possession of the book of Abraham the Jew. He built a laboratory in the château of Rueil, which he often visited to read through the master's manuscripts and to try to interpret the sacred hieroglyphs. But that which a sage like Flamel had been able to understand only after twenty-one years of meditation was not likely to be at once accessible to a statesman like Richelieu. Knowledge of the mutations of matter, of life and death, is more complex than the art of writing tragedies or administering a kingdom. Richelieu's search gave no result.

On the death of the cardinal all traces of the book* were lost, or rather, all traces of the text, for the diagrams have often been reproduced. It must have been copied, for in the seventeenth century the author of the *Trésor des recherches et antiquités gauloises* made a journey to Milan to see a copy which belonged to the Seigneur of Cabrières.

It has now disappeared. Perhaps a copy or the original itself rests under the dust of some provincial library ; and it may be that a wise fate will send it at the proper time to a man who has the patience to ponder it, the knowledge to interpret it, the wisdom not to divulge it.

But the mystery of the story of Flamel, which seemed to have come to an end, was revived in the seventeenth century.

Louis XIV sent an archæologist, named Paul Lucas, on a mission to the East. He was to study antiquities and bring back any inscriptions or documents which might help forward the modest scientific efforts then being made in France. A scholar had in those days to be at the same time both a soldier and an adventurer. Paul Lucas united in himself the qualities of a Salomon Reinach and a Casanova. He was captured by Barbary corsairs, who robbed him, according to his own story, of the treasures he had brought from Greece and Palestine.

* Eliphas Lévi, with the sibylline authoritativeness that is habitual to him, asserts at a venture, without any evidence, that the book of Abraham the Jew is none other than the Ash Mezareph, the commentary on the Cabalistic Sepher Yetzirah.

The most valuable contribution that this official emissary made to science is summarised in the story he tells in his *Voyage dans la Turquie*, which he published in 1719. His account enables men of faith to reconstitute part of the history of the book of Abraham the Jew.

At Broussa Paul Lucas made the acquaintance of a kind of philosopher, who wore Turkish clothes, spoke almost every known language and, in outward appearance, belonged to the type of man of whom it is said that they " have no age." Thanks to his own culture Lucas came to know him fairly well, and this is what he learned. This philosopher was a member of a group of seven philosophers, who belonged to no particular country and travelled all over the world, having no other aim than the search for wisdom and their own development. Every twenty years they met at a pre-determined place, which happened that year to be Broussa. According to him human life ought to have an infinitely longer duration than we admit ; the average length should be a thousand years. A man could live a thousand years if he had knowledge of the philosopher's stone, which, besides being knowledge of the transmutation of metals, was also knowledge of the elixir of life. The sages possessed it and kept it for themselves. In the West there were only a few such sages. Nicolas Flamel had been one of them.

Paul Lucas was astonished that a Turk, whom he had met by chance at Broussa, should be familiar with the story of Flamel. He was still more astonished when the Turk told him how the book of Abraham the Jew had come into Flamel's possession ; for hitherto no one had known this.

"Our sages," he told Lucas, "though there are but few of them in the world, may be met with in any sect. There was a Jew in Flamel's time who had determined not to lose sight of the descendants of his brothers who had taken refuge in France. He had a desire to see them, and in spite of all we could do to dissuade him he went to Paris. He made the acquaintance there of a rabbi who was seeking the philosopher's stone. Our friend became intimate with the rabbi and was able to explain much to him. But before he left the country the rabbi, by an act of black treachery, killed him to get possession of his papers. He was arrested, convicted of this and other crimes and burned alive. The persecution of the Jews began not long afterwards and, as you know, they were expelled from the country."

The book of Abraham, which had been brought by the Eastern sage, was given to Flamel by a Jewish intermediary who did not know its value and was anxious to get rid of it before leaving Paris. But the most amazing thing that Paul Lucas heard was the statement made by the Turk at Broussa that both Flamel and his wife Pernelle were still alive. Having discovered the philosopher's stone he had been able to remain alive in the physical form he possessed at the time of his discovery. Pernelle's and his own funerals and the minute care he bestowed on the arrangements for them had been nothing but clever shams. He had started out for India, the country of the initiates, where he still was.

The publication of Paul Lucas' book created a great sensation. In the seventeenth century, like to-day, there lived discerning men who believed that all truth came out of the East and that there were in India adepts who possessed powers infinitely greater than those which science so parsimoniously metes out to us. For this is a belief that has existed at every period.

Was Nicolas Flamel one of these adepts ? Even if he was, can it reasonably be presumed that he was alive three centuries after his supposed death, by virtue of a deeper study than had yet been made of the life of man and the means of prolonging it ? Is it relevant to compare with Paul Lucas' story another tradition reported by Abbé Vilain, who says that in the seventeenth century Flamel visited M. Desalleurs, the French ambassador to the Sublime Porte ? Every man, according to his feeling for the miraculous, will come to his own conclusion.

I think, myself, that in accordance with the wisdom which he had always shown, Nicolas Flamel, after his discovery of the philosopher's stone, would have had no temptation to evade death ; for he regarded death merely as the transition to a better state. In obeying, without seeking escape, the ancient and simple law which reduces man to dust when the curve of his life is ended, he gave proof of a wisdom which is none the less beautiful for being widespread.

ALCHEMISTS AND ADEPTS

THERE were other adepts after Nicolas Flamel who possessed the secret of the philosopher's stone. We do not know the names of the greatest of them, for the true sign of an adept is his ability to remain unknown. The only trace of them that has come to us is the odour of truth that wisdom leaves behind her. But we know, at any rate partially, the lives of the semi-adepts, who had enough knowledge to practise transmutation, who dimly saw the path to the divine, but remained too human to prevent themselves giving way to their passions. They took part in the work of alchemy with a selfish aim; and since anything to do with gold unlooses greed and hatred, they were carried away by their own folly and almost all of them perished miserably.

About the middle of the sixteenth century an English lawyer named Talbot who was travelling in Wales, stopped for the night at an inn in a little mountain village. He was wearing a curious cap which encircled his head and face down to the chin. The cap was never removed, and was invariably mentioned when descriptions of him were circulated. This strange head-dress served to hide the place where his ears had been—they had just been cut off in London as a punishment for forgery. The inn-keeper of the little inn where he slept was accustomed to show his customers, as a curiosity, an unintelligible old manuscript. He showed it to Talbot, who was quite well aware of the profit sometimes to be derived from old papers and enquired the origin of the manuscript.

It appeared that a few years before, during the religious wars, some Protestant soldiers had rifled the grave of a Catholic bishop, who, during his lifetime, had been a very rich man. In the grave they found this manuscript and two ivory balls, one red and the other white. They broke the red ball and, finding in it nothing but a dark powder, threw it away. The manuscript and the white ball they had left with the inn-keeper in exchange for a few bottles of wine. While the inn-keeper was showing the manuscript his children were playing with the ball.

Talbot suspected something, bought the manuscript and the ball for a guinea, and as he had a friend, a Dr. John Dee, who was interested in hermetic science, he went to see him and showed him his find. Dee realised that the manuscript dealt with the philosopher's stone and with the methods of finding it, but that it did so in a symbolical form the meaning of which escaped him. He opened the white ball and found inside it a powder which was none other than the precious projection powder. With its help he was able at his first experiment in the presence of the astounded Talbot to make gold.

To describe Talbot as being astounded hardly conveys his condition. Most men lose their self-control under the influence of gold; for the royal metal with its dull glitter produces an intoxication which is more intense than that produced by any alcohol. It increases a man's base passions, his desire for physical gratification, avarice, vanity. Gripped by the lust for gold, Talbot made a pact with John Dee, whose help was indispensable to him for the operation of transmutation; and, as his reputation in England was exceedingly bad, a fact of which his cap reminded him at every turn, they began to travel.

The two companions, whose link was lust for gold, went to Bohemia and Germany. John Dee was still unable to understand the Catholic bishop's manuscript, but he could use the powder. The style they kept up and the lectures of Talbot, who boasted of being an adept and of being able to make gold at will, created a great stir wherever they went. The Emperor Maximilian II sent for Talbot and, with his entire court, was present at an attempt at transmutation. He immediately appointed Talbot Marshal of Bohemia. But what he wanted from him was not a small quantity of projection powder, but the secret of its production. He had Talbot watched and then imprisoned him so that the precious secret should not be lost. But Talbot was unable to reveal a secret he did not know, and the stock of the bishop's powder was nearly exhausted.

John Dee, who had been wise enough to realise his own ignorance and remain in obscurity, fled to England, where he sought and received the protection of Queen Elizabeth. The manuscript on which he had laboured seems to have kept its secret until his death, for he lived the last part of his life on a small pension given him by the queen. The arrogant Talbot killed one of his guards in an attempt to escape and died in his prison.

I have told this story to show that the secret of the philosopher's stone was not given to Nicolas Flamel alone, but that it was known from immemorial times, that it filtered through the ages by various means and was received by men in modern times, for their weal or woe, according to their capacity to understand and love their fellow beings.

History records many men who have been able to make gold. But this was only the first stage of the secret. The second gave the means of healing physical illnesses through the same agent which produced transmutation. To reach this stage a higher intelligence and a more complete disinterestedness were necessary. The third stage was accessible only to very few. Just as the molecules of metals are transformed under great increase of temperature, so the emotional elements in human nature undergo an increased intensity of vibrations which transforms them and makes them spiritual. In its third stage the secret of the philosopher's stone enabled a man's soul to attain unity with the divine spirit. The laws of Nature are alike for that which is above and for that which is below. Nature changes according to an ideal. Gold is the perfection of terrestrial substances, and it is to produce gold that minerals evolve. The human body is the model of the animal kingdom, and living forms orientate themselves in the direction of their ideal type. The emotional substance of the soul strives, through the filter of the senses, to transform itself into spirit and return to unity with the divine. The movements of Nature are governed by a single law, which is diverse in its manifestations but uniform in its essence. It was the discovery of this law that the alchemists sought. If there were many of them who discovered the mineral agent, fewer were able to find its application to the human body, and only a very few adepts knew of the essential agent, the sublime heat of the soul, which fuses the emotions, consumes the prison of form and allows entry into the higher world.

Raymond Lulle made gold for Edward III, King of England. George Ripley gave a hundred thousand pounds of alchemical gold to the Knights of Rhodes when they were attacked by the Turks. Gustavus Adolphus of Sweden had an enormous number of gold pieces coined which were marked with a special mark because they were of hermetic origin. They had been made by an unknown man under the protection of the king, who was found at his death to possess a considerable quantity of gold. In 1580 the Elector Augustus of Saxony, who was an alchemist, left a fortune of seventeen million rixdollars. The source of the fortune of Pope John XXII, whose residence was Avignon and whose revenues were small, must be ascribed to alchemy (at his death there were in his treasury twenty-five million florins). This must be concluded also in the case of the eighty-four quintals of gold possessed in 1680 by Rudolph II of Germany. The learned chemist Van Helmont and the doctor Helvetius, who were both of them sceptics with regard to the philosopher's stone and had even published books against it, were converted as a result of an identical adventure which befell them. An unknown man visited them and gave them a small quantity of projection powder; he asked them not to perform the transmutation until after his departure and then only with apparatus prepared by themselves, in order to avoid all possibility of fraud. The grain of powder given to Van Helmont was so minute that he smiled; the unknown man smiled also and took back half of it, saying that what was left was enough to make a large quantity of gold. Both Van Helmont's and Helvetius' experiments were successful, and both men became acknowledged believers in alchemy.*

Van Helmont was the greatest chemist of his day. If we do not hear nowadays that Madame Curie has had a mysterious visitor who gave her a little powder "the colour of the wild poppy and smelling of calcined sea salt," the reason may be that the secret is lost; or, possibly, now that alchemists are no longer persecuted or burnt, it may be that they no longer need the favourable judgment of those in official power.

Until the end of the eighteenth century it was customary to hang alchemists dressed in a grotesque gold robe on gilded gallows. If they escaped this punishment they were usually imprisoned by barons or kings, who either compelled them to make gold or extorted their secret from them in exchange for their liberty. Often they were left to starve in prison. Sometimes they were roasted by inches or had their limbs slowly broken. For when gold is the prize, religion and morality are effaced and human laws set at nought.

This is what happened to Alexander Sethon, called the Cosmopolitan. He had had the wisdom to hide all his life and avoid the company of the powerful. He was a truly wise man. However, he married. In order to please his wife, who was young and beautiful,

* Louis Figuier, *L'alchimie et les alchimistes.*

he yielded to the invitation extended him by the Elector of Saxony, Christian II, to come to his court. As he was unwilling to disclose the secret of the philosopher's stone, which he had long possessed, he was scalded every day with molten lead, beaten with rods and torn with needles till he died.

Michael Sendivogius, Botticher and Paykull spent part of their lives in prison, and many men suffered death for no other crime than the study of alchemy.

If a great number of these seekers were impelled by ambition, if there were among them charlatans and impostors, yet many of them cherished a genuine ideal of moral development. At all events their work in the domain of physics and chemistry formed a solid basis for the few wretched fragmentary scraps of knowledge which are called modern science, and are cause for great pride to a large number of ignorant men.

These men regard the alchemists as dreamers and fools, though every discovery of their infallible science is to be found in the dreams and follies of the alchemists. It is no longer a paradox, but a truth attested by recognised scientists themselves, that the few fragments of truth that we moderns possess are due to the pretended or genuine adepts who were hanged in the Middle Ages with a gilt dunce's cap on their heads.

Moreover, not all of them saw in the philosopher's stone the mere vulgar, useless aim of making gold. A small number of them received, either through a master or through the silence of daily meditation, higher truth.

These were the men who, by having observed it in themselves, understood the symbolism of the third essential rule of alchemy : *Use only one vessel, one fire and one instrument.*

They knew the characteristics of the sole agent, of the secret fire, of the serpentine power which moves upwards in spirals, " of the great primitive force hidden in all matter, organic and inorganic," which the Hindus call *kundalini*, which creates and destroys simultaneously. They calculated that the capacity for creation and the capacity for destruction were equal, that the possessor of the secret had power for evil as great as his power for good ; and just as nobody trusts a child with a high explosive, so they kept the divine science to themselves, or, if they left a written account of the facts they had found, they always omitted the essential point, so that it could be understood only by someone who already knew.

Examples of such men were, in the seventeenth century, Thomas Vaughan, called Philalethes, and, in the eighteenth century, Lascaris. It is possible to form some idea of the lofty thought of Philalethes from his book *Introitus ;* but Lascaris has left us nothing. Little is known of their lives. Both of them wandered about Europe teaching those whom they considered worthy of being taught. They made gold often, but only for special reasons. They did not seek glory, but shunned it. They had knowledge enough to foresee persecution and avoid it. They had neither fixed abode nor family. It is not known when and where they died.

It is probable that they attained the most highly developed state possible to man, that they accomplished the transmutation of their soul. While still living they were members of the spiritual world. They had regenerated their being, performed the task of man. They were twice born. They devoted themselves to helping their fellow-men; this they did in the most useful way, which does not consist in healing the ills of the body or in improving men's physical state. They used a higher method, which in the first instance can be applied only to a small number, but eventually affects all. They helped the noblest minds to reach the goal which they had reached themselves. They sought such men in the towns through which they passed, and, generally, during their travels. They had no school and no regular teaching, because their teaching was on the border of the human and the divine. But they knew that a word sown at a certain time in a certain soul would bring results a thousand times greater than those which could accrue from the knowledge gained through books or ordinary science.

From the bottom of our hearts we ought to thank the modest men who held in their hands the magical formula which makes a man master of the world, a formula which they took as much trouble to hide as they had taken to discover it. For however dazzling and bright the obverse of the medallion, its reverse is dark as night. The way of good is the same as the way of evil, and when a man has crossed the threshold of knowledge, he has more intelligence but no more capacity for love. He is even tempted to have less. For with knowledge comes pride, and egoism is created by the desire to uphold the development of qualities that he considers sublime. Through egoism he returns to the evil which he has tried to escape. Nature is full of traps, and the higher he rises in the hierarchy of men, the more numerous and the better hidden are the traps.

Ascetics are fortunate in so far as their asceticism is in some measure obligatory, in so far as they have not the possibility of satisfying passions which are dormant in them and which they know only from having observed them in others. But how dramatic it would be if the door of their cell should suddenly open and disclose within reach of their hand all that they desire or might have desired! St Anthony in his desert was surrounded by nothing but dreams. He stretched out his arms to grasp them, and if he did not succumb to temptation it was only because the phantoms vanished when he sought to seize them. But the living, almost immediately tangible reality of gold, which gives everything—what superhuman strength would be necessary to resist it! That is what had to be weighed by the adepts who possessed the triple hermetic truth. They had to remember those of their number who had failed and fallen away so lightly. And they had to ponder how apparently illogical and sad for mankind is the law by which the tree of wisdom is guarded by a serpent infinitely more to be feared than the serpent which tempted Eve in the Garden of Eden.

SAINT-GERMAIN THE IMMORTAL

HIS ORIGIN

THERE is a close relationship between the supreme art of the genius and the art of the charlatan. Magicians, sages, Cabalists, initiators, have all unbent at times to perform tricks, to astonish and dazzle the ignorant. From the remotest antiquity the greatest of them have accomplished sham miracles, faked the revelations of oracles, waved magic wands and made every effort to impress the crowd by the pageantry of vestments and the white robes of hierophants. They have done conjuring tricks, made use of the illusion of mirrors, foretold eclipses. Like celebrated actors or fashionable courtesans they have enjoyed being the subject of talk. A similar vanity is to be found in great poets, generals and statesmen. Perhaps it is the inevitable counterpart of genius. Or perhaps men can learn only by the process of being astonished. Many average, reasonable men can conceive wisdom only under the boring form of a sermon, and the sage only in the semblance of a clergyman. For such men prudery, hypocrisy and the most abject enslavement to ritual, habit and prejudice must be daily virtues. When therefore it happens that a genuine sage, by way of amusing himself, mystifies his contemporaries—follows a woman or light-heartedly raises his glass—he is condemned eternally by the army of short-sighted mediocrities whose judgment forms posterity.

That is what happened in the case of the Comte de Saint-Germain. He had a love of jewels in an extreme form, and he ostentatiously showed off those he possessed. He kept a great quantity of them in a casket, which he carried about everywhere with him. The importance he attached to jewels was so great that in the pictures painted by him, which were in themselves remarkable, the figures were covered with jewels; and his colours were so vivid and strange that faces looked pale and insignificant by contrast. Jewels cast their reflection on him and threw a distorting light on the whole of his life.

His contemporaries did not forgive him this weakness. Nor did they forgive him for keeping for an entire century the physical appearance of a man of between forty and fifty years old. Apparently a man cannot be taken seriously if he does not conform strictly to the laws of nature, and he was called a charlatan because he possessed a secret which allowed him to prolong his life beyond known human limits.

He seems also to have been free personally from the solemnity in which men of religion and philosophers wrap themselves. He enjoyed and sought the company of the pretty women of his day. Though he never ate any food in public, he liked dining out because of the people he met and the conversation he heard. He was an aristocrat who lived with princes and even with kings almost on a footing of equality. He gave recipes for removing wrinkles and dyeing hair. He had an immense stock of amusing stories with which he regaled society. It appears from the memoirs of Baron von Gleichen that when Saint-Germain was in Paris he became the lover of Mlle Lambert, daughter of the Chevalier Lambert, who lived in the house in which he lodged. And it appears from Grosley's memoirs that in Holland he became the lover of a woman as rich and mysterious as himself.

At first sight all this is incompatible with the high mission with which he was invested, with the part he played in the secret societies of Germany and France. But the contradiction is perhaps only apparent. His outward appearance of a man of the world was necessary in the first place for the purposes of the secret diplomacy in which Louis XV often employed him. Moreover, we often have an erroneous conception of the activities of a master. The possession of an "opal of monstrous size, of a white sapphire as big as an egg, of the treasures of Aladdin's lamp," is a harmless pleasure if these treasures have been inherited or have been made through the help of miraculous knowledge. It is no great eccentricity in a man to pull down his cuffs in order to show the sparkle of the rubies in his links. And if Mlle Lambert had the ideas of her time on the subject of gallantry, the Comte de Saint-Germain can hardly be reproached for lingering one night in her room in order to open in her presence the mysterious jewel-casket and invite her to choose one of those diamonds which were the admiration of Mme de Pompadour.

For pleasure in life drags a man down only when it is carried to excess. It may be that there exists a way by which a man may attain the highest spirituality and yet keep this pleasure. Moreover, on a certain plane, the chain of the senses no longer exists and kisses cease to burn; a man can no longer harm either himself or others by virtue of the power which the transformation has wrought in him.

* * * * * *

"A man who knows everything and who never dies," said Voltaire of the Comte de Saint-Germain. He might have added that he was a man whose origin was unknown and who disappeared without leaving a trace. In vain his contemporaries tried to penetrate the mystery, and in vain the chiefs of police and the ministers of the various countries whose inhabitants he puzzled, flattered themselves that they had solved the riddle of his birth. Louis XV must have known who he was, for he extended to him a friendship which aroused the jealousy of the court. He allotted him rooms in the château of Chambord. He shut himself up with Saint-Germain and Mme de Pompadour for whole evenings; and the pleasure he derived from his conversation and the admiration he no doubt felt for the range of his knowledge cannot explain the consideration, almost the deference, he had for him. Mme du Housset says in her memoirs that the king spoke of Saint-Germain as a personage of illustrious birth. The Landgrave Charles of Hesse Cassel, with whom he lived during the last years in which history is able to follow his career, must also have possessed the secret of his birth. He worked at alchemy with him, and Saint-Germain treated him as an equal. It was to him that Saint-Germain entrusted his papers just before his supposed death in 1784.

Now, neither Louis XV nor the Landgrave of Hesse Cassel ever revealed anything about the birth of Saint-

Germain. The landgrave even went so far as invariably to withhold the smallest detail bearing on the life of his mysterious friend. This is a very remarkable fact. Saint-Germain was an extremely well-known figure. In those days, when the aristocracy immersed itself in the occult sciences, secret societies and magic, this man, who was said to possess the elixir of life and to be able to make gold at will, was the subject of interminable talk. An inner force which is irresistibly strong compels men to talk. It makes no difference whether a man is a king or a landgrave; all alike are subject to this force, and increasingly subject to it in proportion as they spend their time with women. For Louis XV and the landgrave to have held out against the curiosity of beloved mistresses we must presume in them either a strength of mind that they certainly did not possess or else some imperious motive which we cannot determine.

The commonest hypothesis about his birth is that he was the natural son of the widow of Charles II of Spain and a certain Comte Adanero, whom she knew at Bayonne. This Spanish queen was Marie de Neubourg, whom Victor Hugo took as the heroine of his *Ruy Blas*, regardless of her real character.

Those who disliked Saint-Germain said that he was the son of a Portuguese Jew named Aymar, while those who hated him said, in the effort to add to his discredit, that he was the son of an Alsatian Jew named Wolff.

Fairly recently a new genealogy of Saint-Germain has been put forward, which seems the most probable of all. It is the work of the theosophists and Mrs. Annie

Besant, who has frequently made the statement that the Comte de Saint-Germain was one of the sons of Francis Racoczi II, Prince of Transylvania. The children of Francis Racoczi were brought up by the Emperor of Austria, but one of them was withdrawn from his guardianship. The story was put about that he was dead, but actually he was given into the charge of the last descendant of the Medici family, who brought him up in Italy. He took the name of Saint-Germain from the little town of San Germano, where he had spent some years during his childhood and where his father had estates. This would give an air of probability to the memories of southern lands and sunny palaces which Saint-Germain liked to call up as the setting of his childhood. And it would help to account for the consideration which Louis XV showed him. The impenetrable silence kept by him and by those to whom he entrusted his secret would in this event be due to fear of the Emperor of Austria and possible vengeance on his part. The belief that Saint-Germain and the descendant of the Racoczis are one and the same is firmly held by many people, who regard him as a genuine adept and even think he may still be living. These people have, however, less regard for historical truth than for intuitive knowledge and miraculous revelation.

THE RIDDLE OF HIS LIFE AND DEATH

THE Comte de Saint-Germain was a man " of middle height, strongly built, and dressed with superb simplicity." He spoke with an entire lack of ceremony to the most highly-placed personages and was fully conscious of his superiority. I give Gleichen's account of how he met him for the first time.

" He threw down his hat and sword, sat down in an armchair near the fire and interrupted the conversation by saying to the man who was speaking : ' You do not know what you are saying. I am the only person who is competent to speak on this subject, and I have exhausted it. It was the same with music, which I gave up when I found I had no more to learn.' "

At the court of the Margrave of Anspach, then in extreme old age, he once showed the venerable gentleman a letter he had had from Frederick II and said to him : " Do you know this writing and seal ? "

" Most certainly I do," replied the margrave ; " it is Frederick's seal."

" Quite right," said Saint-Germain ; " but you will never know what the letter says." And he gravely put it back in his pocket.

" He played and composed music with equal ease and with the same success." Many people who heard him play the violin said of him that he equalled or even surpassed the greatest virtuosos of the period ;

and he seems indeed to have justified his remark about himself, that he had reached the extreme limit possible in the art of music.

One day he took Gleichen to his house and said to him :

" I am pleased with you, and you have earned my showing you a few pictures."

" And he very effectively kept his word," says Gleichen ; " for the pictures he showed me all bore a stamp of singularity or perfection which made them more interesting than many pictures of the highest order."

He seems not to have excelled as a poet. There survive of his an indifferent sonnet and a letter addressed to Marie Antoinette (quoted by the Comtesse d'Adhémar) which contains predictions in doggerel verse. At the request of Mme de Pompadour he also wrote a rather poor outline of a comedy. But poetry is an airy grace which seems to be granted by the powers that distribute it, to imperfect beings marked with the fickle quality of emotion ; and inspiration usually comes from its unknown sources only to him who has been vouchsafed little learning.

The greatest obvious talents of the Comte de Saint-Germain were connected with his knowledge of chemistry. If he knew how to make gold he was wise enough to say nothing about it. Nothing but the possession of this secret could perhaps account for the enormous wealth at his command, though he was not known to have money lying at any banker's. What he does seem to have admitted, at least ambiguously, is that he could make a big diamond out of several small stones.

The diamonds which he wore in his shoes and garters were believed to be worth more than 200,000 francs. He asserted also that he could increase the size of pearls at will, and some of the pearls in his possession certainly were of astonishing size.

If all that he said on this subject was mere bragging, it was expensive, for he supported it by magnificent gifts. Mme du Hausset tells us that one day when he was showing the queen some jewels in her presence, she commented on the beauty of a cross of white and green stones. Saint-Germain nonchalantly made her a present of it. Mme du Hausset refused, but the queen, thinking the stones were false, signed to her that she might accept. Mme du Hausset subsequently had the stones valued, and they turned out to be genuine and extremely valuable.

But the feature in Saint-Germain's personality that is hardest to believe is his astounding longevity. The musician Rameau and Mme de Gergy (with the latter of whom, according to the memoirs of Casanova, he was still dining in about 1775) both assert that they met him at Venice in 1710, under the name of the Marquis de Montferrat. Both of them agree in stating that he then had the appearance of a man of between forty and fifty years old. If their recollection is accurate this evidence destroys the hypotheses according to which Saint-Germain was the son of Marie de Neubourg or the son of Francis Racoczi II, for if he had been, he would not have been more than about twenty in 1710. Later, Mme de Gergy told Mme de Pompadour that she had received from Saint-Germain at Venice an elixir which enabled her to preserve, for a long time and without the smallest change, the appearance of a woman of twenty-five. A gift as precious as this could not be forgotten. It is true, however, that Saint-Germain, when questioned by Mme de Pompadour on the subject of his meeting with Mme de Gergy fifty years earlier and of the marvellous elixir he was supposed to have given to her, replied with a smile :

" It is not impossible ; but I confess it is likely that this lady, for whom I have the greatest respect, is talking nonsense."

We can compare with this the offer he made to Mme de Genlis when she was a child :

" ' When you are seventeen or eighteen will you be happy to remain at that age, at least for a great many years ? '

" I answered that I should be charmed.

" ' Very well,' he answered me very gravely ; ' I promise you that you shall.' And he at once spoke of something else."

The period of his great celebrity in Paris extended from 1750 to 1760. Everyone agreed then that in appearance he was a man of between forty and fifty. He disappeared for fifteen years, and when the Comtesse d'Adhémar saw him again in 1775 she declared that she found him younger than ever. And when she saw him again twelve years later he still looked the same.

He deliberately allowed his hearers to believe that his life had lasted inconceivably long. He did not actually say so. He proceeded by allusion. " He diluted the strength of the marvellous in his stories, according to the receptivity of his hearer. When he was telling a fool some event of the time of

Charles V* he informed him quite crudely that he had been present. But when he spoke to somebody less credulous, he contented himself with describing the smallest circumstances, the faces and gestures of the speakers, the room and the part of it they were in, with such vivacity and in such detail that his hearers received the impression that he had actually been present at the scene. 'These fools of Parisians,' he said to me one day, 'believe that I am five hundred years old. I confirm them in this idea because I see that it gives them much pleasure —not that I am not infinitely older than I appear.' "†

Tradition has related that he said he had known Jesus and been present at the Council of Nicæa. But he did not go so far as this in his contempt for the men with whom he associated and in his derision of their credulity. This tradition originates from the fact that Lord Gower, who was a practical joker, gave imitations at his house of well-known men of his time. When he came to Saint-Germain, he imitated his manner and voice in an imaginary conversation which Saint-Germain was supposed to have had with the founder of Christianity, of whom Lord Gower made him say: "He was the best man imaginable, but romantic and thoughtless."

About 1760, an English paper, the *London Mercury*, quite seriously published the following story: The Comte de Saint-Germain presented a lady of his acquaintance, who was concerned at growing old, with a phial of his famous elixir of long life. The lady put the phial into a drawer. One of her servants, a middle-aged woman, thought the phial contained a harmless purge

* 1500–1558.—*Trans.*

† Gleichen.

and drank the contents. When the lady summoned her servant next day, there appeared before her a young girl, almost a child. It was the effect of the elixir.

A few drops more, and I have no doubt the servant would have answered her mistress with infantile screams!

"Has anyone ever seen me eat or drink?" said Saint-Germain, as he was passing through Vienna, to Gräffer, who offered him some Tokay. Everyone who knew him agreed in saying that though he liked sitting down to table with a numerous company, he never touched the dishes. He was fond of offering his intimate friends the recipe of a purge made of senna pods. His principal food, which he prepared himself, was a mixture of oatmeal.

Is it so surprising that the authors of memoirs depict him as retaining the same physical appearance during a whole century? Human life may have a duration infinitely longer than that ordinarily attributed to it. It is the activity of our nerves, the flame of our desire, the acid of our fears, which daily consume our organism. He who succeeds in raising himself above his emotions, in suppressing in himself anger and the fear of illness, is capable of overcoming the attrition of the years and attaining an age at least double that at which men now die of old age. If the face of a man who is not tormented by his emotions should retain its youth, it would be no miracle. Not long ago a London medical periodical reported the case of a woman who at seventy-four had preserved "the features and expression of a girl of twenty, without a wrinkle or a white hair. She had become insane as the result of an unhappy love affair, and her insanity consisted in the perpetual re-living of her last separation from her lover." From her conviction that she was young she had remained young. It may be that a subjective conception of time, and the suppression of impatience and expectation, enable a highly developed man to reduce to a minimum the normal wear and tear of the body.

The Comte de Saint-Germain asserted also that he had the capacity of stopping the mechanism of the human clock during sleep. He thus almost entirely stopped the physical wastage which proceeds, without our knowing it, from breathing and the beating of the heart.

His activity and the diversity of his occupations were very great. He was interested in the preparation of dyes and even started a factory in Germany for the manufacture of felt hats. But his principal rôle was that of a secret agent in international politics in the service of France.

He became Louis XV's confidential and intimate counsellor and was entrusted by him with various secret missions. This drew on him the enmity of many important men, including, notably, that of the Duc de Choiseul, the minister for foreign affairs. It was this enmity which compelled him to leave hurriedly for England in order to escape imprisonment in the Bastille.

Louis XV did not agree with his minister's policy with regard to Austria and tried to negotiate peace behind his back by using Holland as an intermediary. Saint-Germain was sent to The Hague to negotiate there with Prince Louis of Brunswick. M. d'Affry, the French minister in Holland, was informed of this step, and complained bitterly to his minister for foreign affairs that France was carrying on negotiations which did not pass through his hands. The Duc de Choiseul seized his opportunity. He sent M. d'Affry orders to demand the extradition of Saint-Germain, have him arrested by the Dutch Government and sent to Paris. This decision was communicated to the king in the presence of his ministers in council, and Louis, not daring to admit his participation in the affair, sacrificed his emissary. But Saint-Germain received warning just before his arrest. He had time to escape and take ship for England. The adventurer Casanova gives us some details of this escape; he happened to be in a hotel near that in which Saint-Germain was staying, and found himself mixed up in a complicated story of jewels, swindlers, duped fathers and girls madly in love with him—a story, in fact, that was typical of the ordinary course of his life.

According to Horace Walpole's letters Saint-Germain had been arrested in London some years previously on account of his mysterious life. He had been set free because there was nothing against him. Walpole, a true Englishman, came to the conclusion that "he was not a gentleman," because he used to say with a laugh that he was taken for a spy. He was not arrested a second time in England. Not long after this he was found in Russia, where he was to play an important but a hidden part in the revolution of 1762. Count Alexis Orloff met him some years later in Italy and said of him: "Here is a man who played an important part in our revolution." Alexis' brother, Gregory Orloff, handed over to Saint-Germain of his own free will 20,000 sequins, an uncommon action, seeing that Saint-Germain had not rendered him any particular service. At that time he wore the uniform of a Russian general and called himself Soltikov.

It was about this period, the beginning of the reign of Louis XVI, that he returned to France and saw Marie Antoinette. The Comtesse d'Adhémar has left a detailed account* of the interview. It was to her that he turned to obtain access to the queen. Since his flight to England he had not reappeared in France, but the memory of him had become a legend, and Louis XV's friendship for him was well known. It was easy, therefore, for the Comtesse d'Adhémar to arrange a meeting with Marie Antoinette, who immediately asked him if he was going to settle in Paris again.

"A century will pass," was his reply, "before I come here again."

In the presence of the queen he spoke in a grave voice and foretold events which would take place fifteen years later. "The queen in her wisdom will weigh that which I am about to tell her in confidence. The Encyclopedist party desires power, which it will obtain only by the complete fall of the clergy. In order to bring about this result it will upset the monarchy. The Encyclopedists, who are seeking a chief among the members of the royal family, have cast their eyes on the Duc de Chartres. The Duc will become the instrument of men who will sacrifice him when he has ceased to be useful to them. He will come to the scaffold instead of to the throne. Not for long will the laws

* Reproduced in the *Lotus Bleu* for 1899 by Mrs. Cooper Oakley.

remain the protection of the good and the terror of the wicked. The wicked will seize power with blood-stained hands. They will do away with the Catholic religion, the nobility and the magistracy."

"So that only royalty will be left," the queen interrupted impatiently.

"Not even royalty. There will be a bloodthirsty republic, whose sceptre will be the executioner's knife."

It is quite plain from these words that Saint-Germain's ideas were entirely different from those ascribed to him by the majority of historical authors of this period, nearly all of whom see in him an active instrument of the revolutionary movement.

These terrible and amazing predictions filled Marie Antoinette with foreboding and agitation. Saint-Germain asked to see the King, in order to make even more serious revelations; but he asked to see him without his minister, Maurepas, being told of it. "He is my enemy," he said; "and I count him among those who will contribute to the ruin of the kingdom, not from malice but from incapacity."

The king did not possess sufficient authority to have an interview with anybody without the presence of his minister. He informed Maurepas of the interview that Saint-Germain had had with the queen, and Maurepas thought it would be wisest to imprison in the Bastille a man who had so gloomy a vision of the future.

Out of courtesy to the Comtesse d'Adhémar, Maurepas visited her in order to acquaint her with this decision. She received him in her room.

"I know the scoundrel better than you do," he

said ... "He will be exposed. Our police officials have a very keen scent. Only one thing surprises me. The years have not spared me, whereas the queen declares that the Comte de Saint-Germain looks like a man of forty."

At this moment the attention of both of them was distracted by the sound of a door being shut. The comtesse uttered a cry. The expression on Maurepas' face changed. Saint-Germain stood before them.

"The king has called on you to give him good counsel," he said; "and in refusing to allow me to see him you think only of maintaining your authority. You are destroying the monarchy, for I have only a limited time to give to France, and when that time has passed I shall be seen again only after three generations. I shall not be to blame when anarchy with all its horrors devastates France. You will not see these calamities, but the fact that you paved the way for them will be enough to blacken your memory."

Having uttered all this in one breath, he walked to the door, shut it behind him and disappeared. All efforts to find him proved useless. The keen scent of Maurepas' police officials was not keen enough, either during the days immediately following or later. They never discovered what had happened to the Comte de Saint-Germain.

As had been foretold to him, Maurepas did not see the calamities for which he had helped to pave the way. He died in 1781. In 1784 a rumour was current in Paris that the Comte de Saint-Germain had just died in the Duchy of Schleswig, at the castle of the Landgrave Charles of Hesse Cassel. For biographers and historians this date seems likely to remain the official date of his death; certain it is that from that day the mystery in which the Comte de Saint-Germain was shrouded grew deeper than ever.

Secluded at Eckenförn in the landgrave's castle, he gave out that he was tired of life. He seemed care-worn and melancholy. He said he felt feeble, but he refused to see a doctor and was tended only by women. No details exist of his death, or rather of his supposed death. No tomb-stone at Eckenförn bore his name. It was known that he had left all his papers and certain documents relating to Freemasonry to the Landgrave of Hesse Cassel. The landgrave for his part asserted that he had lost a very dear friend. But his attitude was highly equivocal. He refused to give any information about his friend or his last moments, and turned the conversation if anyone spoke of him. His whole behaviour gives colour to the supposition that he was the accomplice of a pretended death.

Although, on the evidence of reliable witnesses, he must have been at least a hundred years old in 1784, his death in that year cannot have been genuine. The official documents of Freemasonry say that in 1785 the French masons chose him as their representative at the great convention which took place in that year, with Mesmer, Saint-Martin and Cagliostro. In the following year he was received by the Empress of Russia. Finally, the Comtesse d'Adhémar reports at great length a conversation she had with him in 1789 in the church of the Récollets, after the taking of the Bastille.

His face looked no older than it had looked thirty

years earlier. He said he had come from China and Japan. "There is nothing so strange out there," he said, "as that which is happening here. . . . But I can do nothing. My hands are tied by someone who is stronger than I. There are times at which it is possible to draw back; others at which the decree must be carried out as soon as he has pronounced it."

And he told her in their broad outlines all the events, not excepting the death of the queen, that were to take place in the years that followed. "The French will play with titles and honours and ribbons like children. They will regard everything as a plaything, even the equipment of the Garde Nationale"—he forgot that he sometimes wore a Russian general's uniform himself.—"There is to-day a deficit of some forty millions, which is the nominal cause of the Revolution. Well! under the dictatorship of philanthropists and orators the national debt will reach thousands of millions."

"I have seen M. de Saint-Germain again," wrote Mme d'Adhémar in 1821; "each time to my amazement. I saw him when the queen was murdered; on the 18th of Brumaire;* on the day following the death of the Duc d'Enghien; in January, 1815; and on the eve of the murder of the Duc de Berry."

Mme de Genlis asserts that she met the Comte de Saint-Germain in 1821 during the negotiations for the Treaty of Vienna; and the Comte de Châlons, who was ambassador in Venice, says he spoke to him there soon afterwards in the Piazza di San Marco. There is

* The day on which Napoleon overthrew the Directoire (November 9th, 1799).—*Trans.*

other evidence, though less conclusive, of his survival. The Englishman Grosley says he saw him in 1793 in a revolutionary prison; and someone else wrote that he was one of the crowd surrounding the tribunal at which the Princesse de Lamballe appeared before her execution.

It seems quite certain that the Comte de Saint-Germain did not die at the place and on the date that history has fixed. He continued an unknown career, of whose end we are ignorant and whose duration seems so long that one's imagination hesitates to admit it.

SECRET SOCIETIES

MANY writers who have studied the Revolution period do not believe in the influence exerted by the Comte de Saint-Germain. It is true that he set up no landmarks for posterity, and even obliterated the traces he had made. He left no arrogant memorial of himself such as a book. He worked for humanity, not for himself. He was modest, the rarest quality in men of intelligence. His only foibles were the harmless affectation of appearing a great deal younger than his age and the pleasure he took in making a ring sparkle. But men are judged only by their own statements and by the merits they attribute to themselves. Only his age and his jewels attracted notice.

Yet the part he played in the spiritual sphere was considerable. He was the architect who drew the plans for a work which is as yet only on the stocks. But he was an architect betrayed by the workmen. He had dreamed of a high tower which should enable man to communicate with heaven, and the workmen preferred to build houses for eating and sleeping.

He influenced Freemasonry and the secret societies, though many modern masons have denied this and have even omitted to mention him as a great source of inspiration.

In Vienna he took part in the foundation of the *Society of Asiatic Brothers* and of the *Knights of Light*, who studied alchemy; and it was he who gave Mesmer his fundamental ideas on magnetism and its applications. It is said that he initiated Cagliostro, who visited him on several occasions in Holstein to receive directions from him, though there seems to be no evidence for this. The two men were to be far separated from one another by opposite currents and a different fate.

The Comtesse d'Adhémar quotes a letter she received from Saint-Germain in which he says, speaking of his journey to Paris in 1789: "I wished to see the work that that demon of hell, Cagliostro, has prepared." It seems that Cagliostro took part in the preparation of the revolutionary movement, which Saint-Germain tried to check by developing mystical ideas among the most advanced men of the period. He had foreseen the chaos of the last years of the eighteenth century and hoped to give it a turn in the direction of peace by spreading among its future promoters a philosophy which might change them. But he reckoned without the slowness with which the soul of man develops and without the aversion that man brings to the task. And he left out of his calculations the powerful reactions of hatred.

All over the country secret societies sprang up. The new spirit manifested itself in the form of associations. Neither the nobility nor the clergy escaped what had become a fashion. There were even formed lodges for women, and the Princesse de Lamballe became grand mistress of one of them. In Germany there were the *Illuminati* and the *Knights of Strict Observance,* and Frederick II, when he came to the throne, founded the sect of the *Architects of Africa.* In France the

Order of the Templars was reconstituted, and Freemasonry, whose grand master was the Duc de Chartres, increased the number of its lodges in every town. Martinez de Pasqually taught his philosophy at Marseilles, Bordeaux and Toulouse; and Savalette de Lange, with mystics such as Court de Gebelin and Saint-Martin, founded the lodge of the *Friends Assembled.*

The initiates of these sects understood that they were the depositaries of a heritage which they did not know, but whose boundless value they guessed; it was to be found somewhere, perhaps in traditions, perhaps in a book written by a master, perhaps in themselves. They spoke of this revealing word, this hidden treasure; it was said to be in the hands of "unknown superiors" of these sects, who would one day disclose the wealth which gives freedom and immortality.

It was this immortality of the spirit that Saint-Germain tried to bring to a small group of chosen initiates. He believed that this minority, once it was developed itself, would, in its turn, help to develop another small number, and that a vast spiritual radiation would gradually descend, in beneficent waves, towards the more ignorant masses. It was a sage's dream, which was never to be realised.

With the co-operation of Savalette de Lange, who was the nominal head, he founded the group of *Philalethes*, or truth-lovers, which was recruited from the flower of the *Friends Assembled.* The Prince of Hesse, Condorcet and Cagliostro were members of this group.

Saint-Germain expounded his philosophy at Ermenonville and in Paris, in the rue Plâtrière. It was a Platonic

Christianity, which combined Swedenborg's visions with Martinez de Pasqually's theory of re-integration. There were to be found in it Plotinus' emanations and the hierarchy of successive planes described by modern theosophists. He taught that man has in him infinite possibilities and that, from the practical point of view, he must strive unceasingly to free himself of matter in order to enter into communication with the world of higher intelligences.

He was understood by some. In two great successive assemblies, at which every masonic lodge in France was represented, the *Philalethes* attempted the reform of Freemasonry. If they had attained their aim, if they had succeeded in directing the great force of Freemasonry by the prestige of their philosophy, which was sublime and disinterested, it may be that the course of events would have been altered, that the old dream of a world guided by philosopher-initiates would have been realised.

But matters were to turn out differently. Old causes, created by accumulated injustices, had paved the way for terrible effects. These effects were in their turn to create the causes of future evil. The chain of evil, linked firmly together by men's egoism and hatred, was not to be broken. The light kindled by a few wise visionaries, a few faithful watchers over the well-being of their brothers, was extinguished almost as soon as it was kindled.

LEGEND OF THE ETERNAL MASTER

NAPOLEON III, puzzled and interested by what he had heard about the mysterious life of the Comte de Saint-Germain, instructed one of his librarians to search for and collect all that could be found about him in archives and documents of the latter part of the eighteenth century. This was done, and a great number of papers, forming an enormous dossier, was deposited in the library of the prefecture of police. The Franco-Prussian War and the Commune supervened, and the part of the building in which the dossier was kept was burnt. Thus once again an "accident" upheld the ancient law which decrees that the life of the adept must always be surrounded with mystery.

What happened to the Comte de Saint-Germain after 1821, in which year there is evidence that he was still alive?

An Englishman, Albert Vandam, in his memoirs, which he calls *An Englishman in Paris,* speaks of a certain person whom he knew towards the end of Louis Philippe's reign and whose way of life bore a curious resemblance to that of the Comte de Saint-Germain. He called himself Major Fraser, lived alone and never alluded to his family. "Moreover he was lavish with money, though the source of his fortune remained a mystery to everyone. He possessed a marvellous knowledge of all the countries in Europe at all periods. His memory was absolutely incredible and, curiously enough, he often gave his hearers to understand that he had acquired his learning elsewhere than from books. Many is the time he has told me, with a strange smile, that he was certain he had known Nero, had spoken with Dante, and so on."*

Like Saint-Germain, Fraser had the appearance of a man of between forty and fifty, of middle height and strongly built. The rumour was current that he was the illegitimate son of a Spanish prince. After having been, also like Saint-Germain, a cause of astonishment to Parisian society for a considerable time, he disappeared without leaving a trace.

Was it the same Major Fraser who, in 1820, published an account of his journey in the Himalayas, in which he said he had reached Gangotri, "the source of the most sacred branch of the Ganges," and bathed in the source of the Jumna ?†

It was at the end of the nineteenth century that the legend of Saint-Germain grew so inordinately. By reason of his knowledge, of the integrity of his life, of his wealth and of the mystery which surrounded him, he might reasonably have been taken for an heir of the first Rosicrucians, for a possessor of the philosopher's stone. But the theosophists and a great many occultists regarded him as a master of the great white lodge of the Himalayas.

The legend of these masters is well known. According to it there live in inaccessible lamaseries in Tibet certain

* *An Englishman in Paris,* by A. D. Vandam. 5th ed., 1892.

† *Journal of a Tour through part of the Snowy Range of the Himālā Mountains and to the Sources of the Rivers Jumna and Ganges.* London, 1820.

wise men who possess the ancient secrets of the lost civilisation of Atlantis. Sometimes they send to their imperfect brothers, who are blinded by passions and ignorance, sublime messengers to teach and guide them. Krishna, the Buddha and Jesus were the greatest of these. But there were many other more obscure messengers, of whom Saint-Germain has been considered to be one.

I believe Mme Blavatsky was the first to mention this possibility. " This pupil of Hindu and Egyptian hierophants, this holder of the secret knowledge of the East," she says of him. " The stupid world has always treated in this way men who, like Saint-Germain, have returned to it after long years of seclusion devoted to study with their hands full of the treasure of esoteric wisdom and with the hope of making the world better, wiser and happier."

Between 1880 and 1900 it was admitted among all theosophists, who at that time had become very numerous, particularly in England and America, that the Comte de Saint-Germain was still alive, that he was still engaged in the spiritual development of the West, and that those who sincerely took part in this development had the possibility of meeting him.

About 1900 Mrs. Cooper Oakley devoted some years of her life to searching for the Comte de Saint-Germain. She even lived for a time near the castle of Kolochvar, in Rumanian Transylvania, where she hoped to find him, on evidence which is unknown to me. But she never found him.

Fairly definite suppositions were also made with regard to the number and hierarchy of the masters scattered through the world to guide men's steps. I do not know on what facts these seductive ideas rest. Saint-Germain was called the Hungarian master on account of his predilection for that country and of his incarnation as a member of the Racoczi family. It was alleged that the master Hilarion,* who had inspired Plotinus and Porphyrius, dictated to Mabel Collins the admirable little book entitled *The Idyll of the White Lotus.* In the name of this master, Hilarion, and with the claim that she is his emissary, a woman calling herself the Blue Star has, during the last few months, founded in California a group called *The Temple Movement.* It has been said that the Venetian master long concentrated his power on Venice, helped to enrich the library of St Mark and directed the actions of Ludovico Cornaro and the alchemist Gualdi. It was said that Serapis inspired Egyptian Gnosticism, and some of these theosophists have gone so far as to allege that the master Jesus then inhabited a physical body living among the Druses of Lebanon. No wonder it was said that these astonishing things would transform the life of a man who acquired this knowledge, provided the capacity for doubt were at the same time removed in him.

The documentation on these points is provided by Leadbeater† and Dr. Annie Besant, and unhappily it is obtained by clairvoyance, which deprives it of most of

* "This master was known under the name of Iamblichus. He was the inspirer and spiritual guide of Plotinus and Porphyrius," says Mr. Lazenby in *The Work of the Masters.* Now Iamblichus was the pupil of Porphyrius, who had himself been the pupil of Plotinus. I note this to show that statements made as to the masters must be accepted with a certain reserve.

† Compare Leadbeater's description of certain of Anna Catherine Emmerich's visions.

its value. It was through these methods of clairvoyance that Leadbeater was able to describe in detail, in so far as that was possible by such means, a centre of initiates in Tibet, where he saw, quite near him, all the great adepts. He thus describes the Comte de Saint-Germain :

"Though he is not especially tall, he is very upright and military in his bearing. His eyes are large and brown and are filled with tenderness and humour, though there is in them a glint of power. . . . His face is olive-tanned. His close-cut brown hair is parted in the centre and brushed back from the forehead. . . . Often he wears a dark uniform with facings of gold lace —often also a magnificent red military cloak—and these accentuate his soldier-like appearance."

But Dr. Besant has been more definite and specific still. In *The Theosophist* for January, 1912, she wrote :

"The master (Racoczi), whom I first saw in 19, Avenue Road, in 1896, had told me that there was a painting of him extant, which I should find."

So apparently Dr. Besant knows the Comte de Saint-Germain personally. She tells us how she found the painting in question in the council-hall of the Knights of Malta in Rome. It was a portrait of Count von Hompesch, Grand Master of the Knights of Malta, who was born in 1744 and died at Montpellier in 1805. He lived, therefore, during the period of Saint-Germain's life which historically is the best known. Logically this should demolish the hypothesis that the portrait of the one can also be the portrait of the other. The portrait of Count von Hompesch and that of Saint-Germain were reproduced in *The Theosophist* and the *Lotus Bleu.* "There can be no possible doubt," says Dr.

Besant; "as may be seen by comparing the picture herewith given, photographed from this painting, with the well-known engraving of the Comte de Saint-Germain." But after examining the two faces with the greatest care, I must confess that I am unable to find any resemblance between them.

I only give these details to show the part played by involuntary illusion, and the contradictions (which perhaps are only apparent) inherent in profound faith.

It is worth comparing what Saint-Germain said to Franz Gröffer* ("I set out to-morrow evening. I shall disappear from Europe and go to the Himalayas.") and the arrival in Tibet of the European traveller at the beginning of the nineteenth century†.

"The brotherhood of Khe-lan was famous throughout the land (Upper Tibet); and one of the most famous brothers was an Englishman who had arrived one day during the early part of this century from the West. . . . He spoke every language, including the Tibetan, and knew every art and science, says the tradition. His sanctity and the phenomena produced by him caused him to be proclaimed a Shaberon‡ after a residence of but a few years. His memory lives to the present day among the Tibetans, but his real name is a secret with the Shaberons alone."§ Might not this mysterious traveller be the Comte de Saint-Germain?

But even if he has never come back, even if he is no longer alive and we must relegate to legend the idea that

* Franz Gröffer, *Memories of Vienna.*

† See reference to Major Fraser on p. 234.—*Trans.*

‡ A reincarnation of Buddha.—*Trans.*

§ H. P. Blavatsky, *Isis Unveiled.*

the great Transylvanian nobleman is still wandering about the world with his sparkling jewels, his senna *tisane* and his taste for princesses and queens—even so it can be said that he has gained the immortality he sought. For a great number of imaginative and sincere men the Comte de Saint-Germain is more alive than he has ever been. There are men who, when they hear a step on the staircase, think it may perhaps be he, coming to give them advice, to bring them some unexpected philosophical idea. They do not jump up to open the door to their guest, for material barriers do not exist for him. There are men who, when they go to sleep, are pervaded by genuine happiness because they are certain that their spirit, when freed from the body, will be able to hold converse with the master in the luminous haze of the astral world.

The Comte de Saint-Germain is always present with us. There will always be, as there were in the eighteenth century, mysterious doctors, enigmatic travellers, bringers of occult secrets, to perpetuate him. Some will have bathed in the sources of the Jumna, and others will show a talisman found in the pyramids. But they are not necessary. They diminish the range of the mystery by giving it material form. The Comte de Saint-Germain is immortal, as he dreamed of being.

CAGLIOSTRO THE CHARLATAN

CAGLIOSTRO "far anticipated the hour marked by fate, penetrated more deeply into the sanctuary of nature and set in motion forces which neither his contemporaries nor many subsequent generations were to know and use."* He was extraordinarily gifted in magical science, a master in the art of transmutation, an amazing prophet through the medium of crystals and young girls. He turned mercury into silver and silver into gold. He practised medicine gratuitously, generously distributed remedies to thousands of invalids, and supported at his own expense many of the poor among them. He easily guessed winning numbers in lotteries and communicated them to a few privileged people. He forgave wrongs done him with unprecedented generosity, and even interceded himself for his worst enemies. He opened his door wide to the humble, while the powerful found him difficult of access. He was noble, disinterested, magnanimous. On events and on human nature he held a broader view than any man of his time, and it is easy to understand why his disciples called him Cagliostro the divine.

And yet no one was ever more hated, more betrayed, more despised, than Cagliostro the divine. In London he was robbed and arrested as a swindler. In Paris he

* Mark Haven, *The Unknown Master*.

was involved in the affair of the diamond necklace,* though he had had nothing to do with it, and was confined in the Bastille for several months. In Rome he was sold by his wife, whom he never ceased to love passionately, imprisoned by the Inquisition, tortured and condemned to death. And, which was perhaps worst of all, the Inquisition incited a Jesuit named Marcello to publish, under the title *Life of Joseph Balsamo*, an amazing memorial of hatred and calumny, on which an ignorant posterity has for a century and half based its judgment.

What was the reason for his incomprehensible destiny ? It was that never in the heart of man have such contradictory elements been united. His words were often admirable, but sometimes they were ridiculous. When he was asked in the necklace trial who he was, he replied, " I am a noble traveller." He could not flatter, but he liked to be flattered, and his pride was inordinate. " I was not born of the flesh and of the will of man ; I was born of the spirit," he said. He adored his wife, but deceived her, excusing himself by saying that man's superiority does not lie in living the life of a monk ;

* The affair of the diamond necklace created a tremendous stir in France just before the Revolution. The facts were these :—Cardinal de Rohan, who was anxious to obtain the friendship of Marie Antoinette, allowed himself to be duped by an intriguing woman, the Comtesse de la Motte. This woman made him believe that the queen was longing to have a diamond necklace worth over a million and a half francs, which the king had refused to give her. The cardinal accordingly bought the necklace from a firm of jewellers and gave it to the comtesse to give to the queen. However, the necklace disappeared, the cardinal was unable to pay, and the whole affair came to light. The scandal was exaggerated by the malice of the public and was not without its effect in bespattering the queen, though she was entirely innocent in the matter. —*Trans.*

and he often urged her to become the mistress of other men. He usually dressed simply, but when in Russia he wore the uniform of a Spanish colonel, and the Spanish chargé d'affaires had to insert a notice in a newspaper to the effect that there had never been a colonel of the name of Cagliostro in the Spanish army. He produced the faces of angels in a crystal, and also scenes prophetic of the future. For this purpose he used children dressed in white, and was accustomed to strike them on the forehead with a naked sword; and sometimes he gave them their cue by describing in advance the scenes he wanted them to see when he invoked his tutelary genius. When he gave séances he had skulls, stuffed monkeys and snakes in jars set out on an altar.* The ritual of Egyptian masonry, which he founded, betokens the highest spiritual level and purports to be a religion above all religions. But when he was at Trent with a bigoted prince-bishop, from whom he wanted to get letters of recommendation, he went to confession and communion and, on going home after confession, said to Lorenza: "I've taken in that priest nicely." He healed most of the sick people whom he treated, but his elixir of life, based on Malvoisie wine, was nothing but an aphrodisiac made by distilling the secretions of certain animals with certain herbs.† He spoke several languages fluently, but expressed himself correctly in none of them, even in Italian, his mother tongue. He asserted that he had been brought up in Mecca and made Arabic quotations in the presence of people who did not know Arabic; when, however,

* Antonio Benedetti, *Mémoires*.

† Eliphas Lévi claimed that he had the recipe for this mixture.

on one occasion he was addressed in that language, he did not answer and seemed very much embarrassed.

The perpetual duality of his life showed itself in another way. During the first part of his life he called himself Joseph Balsamo; and Joseph Balsamo was a swindler, a forger and a trickster, who complaisantly turned to his own account the love affairs of his wife Lorenza. From 1777 onwards he called himself the Comte de Cagliostro, and a marvellous genius suddenly descended on him. He was rich, and distributed money open-handedly; he was a doctor—which he had not been before—and effected cures which men thought miraculous; he was a philosopher, and dreamed of the physical and moral regeneration of man.

What had happened? Whence came his extraordinary powers, his medical knowledge, his unquestioned superiority, which dazzled all who met him? He might have been another man. Yet he was the same man. Cagliostro could not disown Joseph Balsamo, though he tried to do so in Paris during his defence at the necklace trial, when he childishly gave himself out to be the natural son of a princess of Trebizond, brought up as a prince at an Arabian Nights court. An unbreakable physical tie united the adventurer Balsamo with the master Cagliostro. He married his wife Lorenza in Rome when he was Balsamo and went on loving her when he became Cagliostro. In vain did he lead a life of perfect disinterestedness dominated by love of humanity. He was pursued by his past. The former man was the perpetual companion of the new man and shadowed the brilliance of his actions.

The riddle of this dual personality has never been solved.

I shall not tell here the story of Cagliostro, richly though it deserves the telling, and I mention his two phases only because " it is impossible to speak of the Comte de Saint-Germain without speaking of him." The two have often been confused, and episodes in the life of the one have been attributed to that of the other, although between the jewel-loving adept and the amorous magician there is in reality only a distant relationship. Each of them formed part, on different sides, of the two opposing currents which divided secret societies at the end of the eighteenth century, then neutralised one another, and resulted finally in the struggle between the Convention and the Jacobins.

Cagliostro was not a messenger, as he asserted with so much pride. " One day I received the grace of being admitted, like Moses, into the presence of the Eternal." But he was one of those bearers of truth, those independent initiators, whom the Roman Church, throughout the centuries, has given itself the task of torturing and burning.

If he saw clearly, in a bottle of water, the fall of the Bastille some months before it took place, he was unable to see in the eyes of his wife Lorenza the treachery which was to deliver him up to the tribunal of the Inquisition. If he charmed and dazzled the Grand Master of the Knights of Malta, Pinto, Cardinal de Rohan and many others, he spoke of God blasphemously before the cardinals assembled to judge him and before the pope, crouching behind a wire screen in the tribunal in order to watch his prisoner rear up the hydra head of Freemasonry.

He was only an imperfect master, a man divided

between aspiration for the divine, the trickery of the charlatan, and the possession of a woman's body. But at least in his death he equalled the greatest. Like Giordano Bruno he was condemned to be burnt. If he did not actually mount the stake, it was because Pope Pius VI, who had personally ordered that an iron collar and manacles should be put on him,* commuted his punishment to perpetual imprisonment in order that his torture might be the more protracted; and the judgment added the words, *without hope of pardon.*

Without hope of pardon, in the penitent's cloak, barefoot, holding a candle, he passed through the streets of Rome between two lines of monks to ask God's forgiveness for his sins. Without hope of pardon he was taken down to an underground cell in the fortress of San Leo. But his implacable ecclesiastical executioners by their very mercilessness gave him the greatness which he had glimpsed but never attained in his lifetime. Without hope of pardon he died in his prison, which the French entered in 1797, too late to set him free.

Now, with the lapse of time, his true rôle is shrouded in obscurity. But the unjust judges, who have always condemned to death initiates and sages, at least contributed to his glory by their tortures and injustice.

* Borowski, *Cagliostro.*

MADAME BLAVATSKY AND THE THEOSOPHISTS

THE MASTERS AND THE CHOICE OF A MESSENGER

WHEN Jacob Boehme was a child he was alone one day in the shop of his father, who was a bootmaker, when an unknown man came in to buy some shoes. He looked deep into the boy's eyes and said solemnly to him :

" Jacob, your words will one day astonish the world. You will have to suffer much from misfortune and persecution ; but never fear and be steadfast, for you are loved of God, and He has pity on you."

Similarly, Helena Petrovna Blavatsky, as she sat in the silent rooms of the house of the Fadeëvs, in which the years of her childhood were spent, sometimes saw about her a shadow, the protecting form of a man, who smiled kindly on her and whose influence she felt upon her. The shadow might have said to her also : " You will have to suffer much from misfortune and persecution." Some people are marked out in advance. Those who receive the mission of bringing to mankind a revelation, a message that liberates the highest faculties of the soul, can do so only at the price of their fellows' hatred. They have to suffer misfortune and persecution. But they form links in a fraternal chain, and from their childhood signs are given to them. Happy the child who is given, by a solemn presence, fugitive as a dream, the promise of a life of suffering, the child to whom it is said: "Never fear and be steadfast, for you are loved of God."

H. P. Blavatsky was the most direct of the messengers of the East of whom we have any knowledge. In the fourteenth century, Tsong Ka Pa, the great sage of India and the reformer of Buddhism, reminded the wise men of the great Tibetan plateaus and the Himalayas of a very ancient law. This law concerned the balance of two opposing principles which are both equally true: *The truth must be kept secret*, and *The truth must be divulged.* For though man is eternally dying as the result of his ignorance, yet knowledge that is prematurely given is as fatal to him as light to a man who has lived long in darkness. Tsong Ka Pa reminded them that at the end of each century an attempt had to be made to teach the West, which cared for nothing but power and material well-being.

In the lamasery of Ghalaring Tcho, near Tzigatzi, on the borders of China and Tibet, certain men who had attained a high spiritual level by meditation, ascetic philosophers, who had raised themselves above our plane by their knowledge and goodness, took counsel as to what intermediary they should employ to bear the message to the unbelieving and arrogant peoples. It appears from what it is possible to know of their deliberation that, by an almost unanimous decision, they were on the point of giving up the attempt. Had not the West lost all possibility of receiving and understanding the true and ancient doctrine? What was the good of sending the message to those who had no desire to receive it?

However, two voices were raised in favour of obedience

to the words of Tsong Ka Pa, the voices of two Hindus: Morya, the descendant of the princes of the Punjab, and Koot Houmi, who was born in Kashmir. They assumed responsibility for the task of sending to the West someone who should diffuse the Brahman philosophy and unveil that part of the mystery of man and nature which it seemed opportune to unveil.

And it was H. P. Blavatsky upon whom their choice fell. Why should it have fallen on her rather than on a man better equipped by balance, powers of persuasion and absence of passion, qualities which were always lacking in H. P. Blavatsky? The answer is connected with a truth which, for all its simplicity, is rejected with a contemptuous smile by men of "common-sense." We are born with a long past. It is this past which determines the conditions and events of our life, whilst we insist on ascribing them to the shadow of hazard, to the phantom of free will. It was in virtue of this past that H. P. Blavatsky was bound to Morya. She was chosen for her extraordinary mediumistic gifts, for the supernormal faculties which she manifested from childhood, for the facility with which Morya and Koot Houmi could communicate with her at a distance by means of thought-telegraphy. And above all, she was chosen for her unselfish faith, her boundless love of knowledge, that mysterious enthusiasm which impels certain people to raise ever higher, though their death should be the result, the living lamp of their intelligence amid the darkness in which it has pleased Nature to envelop us.

* * * * * *

If the existence of the masters is regarded in India, Tibet and China as unquestionable, there is in Europe only a small minority which believes in it; and moreover that minority is not taken seriously by the average cultured man. The reason for this is that there exist no definite facts with regard to the masters, that no material proof of their existence can be given. Such a proof might be found, but it would be necessary to search for it, and the means to be employed would seem unusual. It is more convenient to deny it. Besides, the existence of the masters shocks the pride of the intellectual upstart which each of us brings into the world with him at birth.

The idea that in the sand and snow of a territory reputed barbarous there exist men—and men of colour!—who do not unreservedly admire motor-cars, aeroplanes and the work of medical institutes, but who have nevertheless gone farther than we have in metaphysical knowledge and the study of spiritual matters—such an idea seems unlikely, causes annoyance or a shrug of the shoulders. We are incapable of presuming the existence of higher men without at the same time presuming that they are bound to make a display of their superiority in order to become famous, to gain decorations, to enter official academies! We have reached a point at which disinterestedness is unimaginable to us. It is also unimaginable that anyone should be able to dispense with the marvellous discoveries of science, which have been so cleverly utilised for physical enjoyments. So we liken the sages of Tibetan lamaseries to fakirs who perform easy miracles and mortify their flesh.

On the other hand, those who believe in the masters form an erroneous conception of them. No sooner have they admitted the idea that higher beings exist, withdrawn in solitudes, who are more spiritual than we, who know more, who are more developed—than they ascribe to them the virtue and the power of gods. They forsake probability in order to satisfy a long suppressed feeling for religion, an innate desire for the worship of the divine. For such men not only do the masters possess faculties which the imagination cannot grasp, but they direct humanity at their will, bring about the birth and death of races, read at a glance all the thoughts of all men, weigh good and evil. The legend of the king of the world is exceeded by these believers, who are as blind as the blindest Christians and utterly oblivious of reason. Saint Yves d'Alveydre asks us to believe* that the members of Agharta in their subterranean explorations of the earth have found a race of men with wings and claws and a flying dragon half-man and half-monkey. And Leadbeater† practically summarises the conversations that take place between Jesus and the Buddha on a stone bench at the foot of a great tree.

The masters exist, but they are not gods. They are only men filled with wisdom. That is a great deal. If, as travellers report, they are able to create in themselves artificial heat to resist the cold of the heights, they are yet human enough to suffer from the icy winds and the snow. They are doomed to the regularity of food, to the oblivion of sleep. They feel the hardness of the

* *Mission de l'Inde.*

† *The Masters and the Path.*

earth, the immensity of the heavens, the rigour of natural law. They know the secret of death and can postpone death, but they are nevertheless obliged to submit to it. If they have succeeded in getting rid of the greater part of our sufferings, created by desire and egoism, it may be that they feel other sufferings, of an order that is inconceivable to us, born of their understanding and their love. When they reach the gates of Nirvana, the look they throw behind them at their brothers, who have remained so far away, reveals that which often must cause them to retrace their steps. They conquer pity by intelligence, and by pity they break the diamond of intelligence. But do they attain perfect serenity ?

The summit which they have so painfully gained is no summit. There is no summit in a hierarchy without end. Freed from the social life and its yoke, they see, they know, by the impetus of intuition they reach regions of light ; but even if they wish, they cannot again put on the abandoned yoke. They have cast it behind them. Prisoners who have been set free may not enter their former prison. They are not adapted to men's conduct, to their finesse, their trickery. Not one of these sublime adepts of Agharta could hold a commercial post, be president of an association, or get himself elected deputy. If they have in some measure the capacity to foresee coming events, their calculations must often be put out by the reactions of hatred. If their enlarged intelligence penetrates cosmic laws and possesses powers unknown to us, error must be their lot in the domain of human affairs.

However great the feelings of veneration or awe with which we surround the great messengers, we are compelled to recognise the fact of this error. We can see their powerlessness against evil, the futility of their efforts to maintain their work. We can see that often they have employed childish methods to bring great designs into being. This was the case with the foundation of the theosophical movement, which might have created a moral revolution such as had never been seen. From it might have arisen a hearth of brotherhood, by the fire of which races and religions would have become reconciled to one another. But it was based on error. Its point of departure as a means of propaganda rested on error. It was impossible to found a great movement with phenomena and miracles, even if behind them lay the solid weight of doctrine. It was going too far in misunderstanding the flower of Western minds. Few though they might be, it was these minds whom it was necessary to win over. Though they did not possess true spiritual qualities, they expected something better than the miraculous sending of letters, and roses, still wet with dew, falling from the ceiling. The philosophy of the East was given them with fakir's tricks and the illusions of hallucination. The message lost its grandeur, and ignorant men and sceptics took the opportunity of decrying it.

Men of common-sense refused to admit that a sublime thought could come out of a conjurer's hat. And when *The Secret Doctrine* was published, it was too late. The extraordinary currents of hatred which are unleashed against the revealers of new truths had beset the book and its author. Calumny had attached the label of impostor to H. P. Blavatsky—the sincerest and most disinterested of all who have dedicated their life to the spirit.

H. P. BLAVATSKY'S PHENOMENAL LIFE

THERE has never been a great figure about whom there is not something of the caricature. The gift of the spirit is always matched by some physical disproportion, something ridiculous, some ugliness of feature. The ears of Lao Tse were immoderately long; Socrates' head was too big; Swedenborg was a giant in stature. Moreover, a genius is always ill-adapted to life, inappropriate, embarrassing. He knocks furniture over, has moments of strange dumbness or else expresses himself in a voice which resounds like a clarion.

Thus H. P. Blavatsky is seen as possessing more defects than obvious good qualities. She grew prematurely to an enormous size and carried her defective and tormented body untiringly throughout the four quarters of the world. She overflowed with passion, was perpetually angry; she lost her temper, continually cursed and ordered people about, swore like a trooper; she smoked all day long in public, even in the sacred temples of India, and treated her fraternal comrade Olcott like a fool. At the slightest illness she wrote letters beginning: "I write on my death-bed," and recovered the same day. She was a sleep-walker. She had bohemian tastes. Whether she was in New York or in India she would ask people to dinner on days when she had not even a cup of tea to offer them. She promised everyone, even servants, that they should succeed her as moving spirit of the Theosophical Society. She confided in strangers. She said she knew men's inmost nature through " occult intuition," and gave her friendship to people who sought it only to betray her. With some money that she had inherited she bought some land in America; but she lost the deeds which proved the purchase and even forgot in what district the land was. While she was editing *The Theosophist* in London she founded a paper which competed with *The Theosophist,* and herself assumed the editorship. From horror of religious hypocrisy she became anti-clerical. Wherever she went she made enemies owing to her incapacity to disguise the truth. She was in revolt against every authority, every prejudice, every worldly convention. She respected nothing and nobody, save the masters; and about them she made jokes and called Morya familiarly " the general." But she was generous; she gave all she had. Her only aim in life was her mission, and to perform it she was able to efface herself entirely. She regarded her person merely as the vehicle of expression of higher beings, her voice as the means of proclaiming their message; and to this she subordinated her whole life.

* * * * * *

It was to the sound of the hammering of coffins that H. P. Blavatsky was born, in 1831, near Odessa. Russia was being ravaged by cholera, and several people had just died in the household of her father, Colonel Hahn.

As she was a puny child she was baptised hurriedly. During the ceremony, for which members of the family and serfs were assembled in a large room, a candle carried by a child set a priest's robe alight. There was a panic. The priest was badly burned, and as a result the prediction was made that the child's life would be full of struggle and vicissitude. The prediction came true. But no one then could foresee that Helena Petrovna would re-light the candle of her baptism and, by proclaiming to man the worship of the God within him, would by her words burn many priestly robes and the ornaments of many useless ceremonies.

However far those who knew her as a child go back in their memory, they agree unanimously that at a very early age she showed superhuman capacities. Mysterious knockings took place when she entered a room. She described in advance distant events which took place according to her description. The world about her was peopled with phantoms and spirits whose form she depicted and whose intentions she understood. If she took up a handful of sand from the steppe, she saw the oceans of vanished epochs, submarine flora, fantastic animals. If she looked at an old man passing by, she saw in the atmosphere about him every action that he had done in his previous lives. A master watched over her, he who was later to be known under the name of Morya. One day when her horse bolted and threw her, she felt two invisible arms hold her up and break her fall.

The invisible arms were real arms, the dream figure became a living figure; and when she went to London for the first time she recognised the familiar apparition in the person of one of the Indian rajahs who constituted an embassy from Nepal. She spoke with her master in Hyde Park, and from that moment all her actions were subordinated to his orders. Obviously none of those orders would run counter to her fate. With toil and suffering she would have to work out her own instruction, endure the effects resulting from her impulsive, unruly nature. Her mission was to be carried out amid anxiety, illness and anger; for all messengers are tainted with imperfection, and it is evident that the highest and the best in the hierarchy of creation are liable to weakness and error.

At eighteen she allowed herself to be married by her family to an old general; but she already felt an irresistible horror of what she called the "magnetism of sex," a horror which made her remain chaste all her life. Her old husband did not succeed in kissing even her finger-tips, and she left the conjugal roof at night on horseback.

She began then a series of interminable travels.

After wandering about Egypt and Syria, she went to South America, where she shared the wild life of the cowboys. She travelled to India by the Pacific and made an attempt to penetrate into Tibet, but was prevented by the British Government. She returned to Europe, going by Egypt, where she studied magic with the old Coptic magician Metamon. She became violently interested in the independence of nations and joined the troops of Garibaldi, in whose ranks she received a severe wound. She recovered, read Fenimore Cooper's novels, fell in love with the Redskins and left on the spot for Canada, to live in wigwams, shoot arrows, see scalps. But the squaws stole from her a pair of boots to which she was attached, and she tired of the Redskins and went to live in Texas with the trappers. She soon left Texas and visited New Orleans to penetrate the secrets of voodoo magic. She lived for some time among this sect of negro magicians, but, receiving warning in a dream that she was in danger, she set off again for India. She tried once more to enter Tibet, travelled in the Himalayas, stayed in various Buddhist monasteries. She was frozen by the snow, blinded by the sand, suffered hunger and thirst in tents, and returned to India in 1857, just before the Mutiny. Her occult guide instructed her then to go back to Europe, and she returned to her family, which she proceeded to astound, for some years, by working wonders of every kind. It was not till ten years later that the time of her true instruction came. All her travels had been but a preparatory pastime. She returned to India in 1867, the period of her initiation in Tibet.

She reached Lake Palti and the Kwen Luen Mountains, and in that unexplored region, though she would never say exactly where, she found Morya and Koot Houmi and learned from them the secret knowledge which it was to be her mission to reveal. She was ordered to go to America, where she would find a man whom she did not know, but who had been chosen for his faith, his courage and his unselfish love of good, to found with her the spiritual movement which was to be known under the name of the Theosophical Movement.

She passed through Europe on her way, but catastrophes were in her star: the ship in which she travelled carried a cargo of gunpowder which exploded, and she came near being the sole survivor of the wreck.

As soon as she arrived in America she asked everyone she met whether they knew Colonel Olcott. But she did not have to look for him long. At some party, which she was attending, a man with a long beard offered her a match for a cigarette she had just rolled. The little flame that flashed between them grew into a great spiritual fire, which is not yet extinguished. The tall, quiet, great-hearted American and the indomitable Russian with her unwieldy body, who by her mediumistic faculties could see some part of the beyond, became inseparable knights of the ideal. They were Don Quixotes on the march for the reform of humanity, and under the helmet of their faith, more enchanted than Quixote's helmet of Mambrino,* they fought and conquered the terrible windmills of stupidity and bigotry.

Mme Blavatsky's knowledge of occult science had grown during her travels. She came into contact with every hypnotist, necromancer and sorcerer in the world. With her extraordinary powers she caused equal astonishment to charlatans, men of common-sense and men of learning. There were discussions, explanations, lawsuits. In face of the accumulated facts it is impossible to deny her powers, or if one denies them it is necessary to presume conspiracy on the part of every household which she entered, and complicity on the part of every person whom she met in every part of the world. The phenomena she produced are absolutely astounding. It seems that in certain circumstances and in certain states she had the power to create at will material objects, to write long letters without hand or pen and send them

* Mambrino was a Moorish king in the *Orlando* of Boiardo, whose helmet was won by Rinaldo. Cervantes mentions it in *Don Quixote*, Bk. I, chap. X.—*Trans.*

to a distant destination by means of astral force. She gave another explanation of her own powers. She said she had the power of making herself obeyed by certain spirits intermediate between man and nature, called *elementals;* and she made these magic slaves work for her invisibly.

A child came to visit her in a room that was almost bare. Wishing to give the child pleasure, she put her arm behind a screen and drew out a lamb on wheels, which was not there a minute before.

Another child wanted a whistle. She took three keys attached to a ring and closed her hand on them. When she opened her hand the three keys had become a whistle.

At a dinner it was found that there were no sugar-tongs. She miraculously made a pair, which were slightly out of shape and bore the mark of her masters.

Somebody asked her one day to draw the portrait of an Indian sage, a teacher of outcastes, known by the name of Tiruvalluvar and living at Vilapur. She took a little blacklead, crushed it lightly on a sheet of paper and folded the paper over. One minute later a detailed portrait had been drawn, and the American portrait-painters to whom it was shown declared that from the technical point of view it was a unique work which no living artist could have executed.

On another occasion she was hemming napkins. Colonel Olcott saw her give an irritable kick under the table as she said: " Come out of there, you fool! " He asked what there was there. " It's a little fool of an elemental pulling my skirt," said Mme Blavatsky. " Give him your napkins to hem," said Olcott by way of joke. She threw the napkins under the table, and when they were picked up a quarter of an hour later the hemming was done.

Stories of this kind could be multiplied indefinitely.

These phenomena aroused great curiosity. Mme Blavatsky's reputation became enormous. The Theosophical Society was founded by her and Olcott, and the two of them transferred the headquarters first to Madras and then to Adyar.

Mme Blavatsky had known for some years that her dream was realised. She was in the fullness of her activities. From every part of Europe came adherents to the new faith, to theosophical ideas, which only express the philosophy of certain Buddhist groups in Tibet. With the Buddhist philosophy Mme Blavatsky connected the ideas of evolution and of the attainment of perfection, also an explanation of the creation of the universe which is more ancient than Buddhism and is probably Brahminical in origin. If many Indians proved indifferent to her ideas, a great number became enthusiastic adherents.

But the eternal enemies of every great upspringing of truth took alarm and acted hurriedly. If one reads the books and papers of this period one is amazed at the incredible outburst of hatred provoked by a disinterested group preaching human brotherhood and the cult of truth. And this hatred seemed to be the greater because it was vented on a woman.

It was impossible for the missionaries of the Roman Catholic Church in Madras to tolerate the idea that neighbourly love should be taught by other Europeans than themselves, and in the name of a prophet who was not their prophet. They prepared the work of calumny by which the Roman Church, in forms that vary but are always inexorable, has ever struck at those who preach the divine word outside their own iron rule. They bribed two former boarding-house keepers, who, by the indiscretion of Mme Blavatsky, had become confidential servants at Adyar, to bring a charge of fraud against the founder of the theosophical movement. They alleged that they had been her accomplices, and produced forged letters. According to their story, Mme Blavatsky's phenomena were mere matters of sleight of hand, the masters were shams, there were no masters, there was nothing.

At the same time the Society for Psychical Research in London had sent out to Madras a young man named Hodgson, who possessed full powers and plenty of complacency, to hold an enquiry into the nature of the phenomena produced by Mme Blavatsky. Influenced by the missionaries, by the opinion of conventional English society, which with one voice followed the missionaries, and by his own disinclination to believe, which he had brought out from England in his narrow, sceptical mind, Hodgson declared, in the course of a long report, for Mme Blavatsky's imposture.

The slanders of her enemies were not to be forgotten. They germinated and fructified; for ignorance, false knowledge and materialism found in them a pretext for doubt and the joy of hating what they could not understand. Many of Mme Blavatsky's friends left her and spread fresh slanders. It was said that she was a spy in the service of Russia, and in France Dr. Papus fabricated bodily, without the slightest evidence, the charge that she had copied part of her books from manuscripts left by a certain Baron von Palmes. This charge was grotesque, and the man who brought it knew that it was grotesque. The baron was a former officer in the Austrian cavalry, an ill-educated man and anything but a philosopher, and he had never written a line in his life. The hatred of those who aspire to spiritual supremacy unlooses a frenzy that is blinder than the possession of money.

Mme Blavatsky did not take proceedings against her calumniators. She was poor and could not afford a costly law-suit—a fact of which her enemies were well aware. Besides, she could have given a victorious reply only by proving the actual existence of Morya and Koot Houmi and naming the place where they lived, which she did not wish to do on any account.

Exhausted and ill she left India, in order to find in Europe, in solitude, the quiet necessary for the writing of *The Secret Doctrine*. In a wretched room in Naples she tasted the bitterness of seeing her best intentions disparaged, her work denied, her ideal flouted. But no doubt from the deep inner resources which great souls possess she drew the idea that the written word is more important than the person entrusted with the writing of it, and that the book survives long after the face and even the name of the author have passed into oblivion. She subordinated her life to the making of her book. She forgot the powers by means of which she had gathered admirers round her. She ceased producing snakes out of hand-bags and many-coloured butterflies by a gesture. She spent the last years of her life with her eyes fixed on the deepest sources of her knowledge. She stood out against the waves of hatred implicit in newspaper articles or in the poisoned words of those who came to visit her. Her health was precarious, but she pursued her aim unfalteringly by sheer force of will, compelling herself to do some of her great work every day.

When she died in England she had once more found disciples and friends who loved her. She liked to repeat the words of Vishnu Purana : *Pity is the strength of the virtuous.* She was able quietly to contemplate her finished task. She had written the last words of *The Secret Doctrine*, and the Theosophical Society had spread all over the world.

But since it is a bitter and inexorable law that calumny, skilfully directed, leaves a trace that does not die, Mme Blavatsky has never been altogether cleared of the accusations brought against her. The years have passed, and the origins and proofs of bygone events soon become uncertain. People listen to rumour, which is easily mistaken for a lower form of wisdom. With secret pleasure they breathe the breath of a scandal whose origin is unknown. They say to themselves : " After all, who knows ? It may be true. . . ." And even those who believe the most firmly in Mme Blavatsky and have received the truest consolation from her philosophy sometimes feel a doubt rise from the depths of their being, like a melancholy cloud casting a shadow.

In the complete text of the Jewish historian, Josephus, which was recently found in Russia, there is a striking passage. This contemporary of John the Baptist and of Jesus writes with regard to John the Baptist : " He placed the skins of animals on those parts of his body which were hairless." So this prophet added to nature in order to carry out his idea of the appearance of a prophet. And I imagine that he did so secretly in order that, in the eyes of his disciples, he might appear an emissary, whom God had created hairy, by contrast with the luxurious clothing of the rich Jews. It was a childish action on his part; yet he was John the Baptist, who baptised Jesus.

Similarly Mme Blavatsky, who had been given the gift of producing phenomena and perhaps considered that she could not be a genuine wonder-worker without continual phenomena, may have made additions of her own invention by guile and artifice; for it must have been a great temptation to help on a miracle when it did not take place of its own accord, and when she nevertheless bore within herself a miracle, which she performed yesterday and would perform again to-morrow. It is possible that Mme Blavatsky yielded to this temptation, though there is no proof of it. However, the whole matter is unimportant. If the prophet wishes to be hairy, let him be hairy to his heart's content. The baptismal water between the banks of Jordan will not be the less clear for that. It matters nothing to me if the person who gives me a reasonable explanation of the world, a lofty philosophy, and a morality which transforms my heart, magically spirits away the book which contains the sublime explanation, philosophy and morality. I check my astonishment at the brilliance of the trick, wait for the book to reappear, and then drink in its revealing wisdom without bothering about the miraculous manner in which it was presented to me.

THE SECRET DOCTRINE

THE characteristic of the philosophy taught by H. P. Blavatsky is that it appears to many minds, when revealed to them, as the noblest of all philosophies, as the only system which is clear and reasonable, and the knowledge of which is a motive to self-development.

To become more intelligent and better, not in the ordinary meaning of the words, but to become more worthy of esteem in one's own eyes—that is what is possible for man nowadays, thanks to her. On those who have found the truth appropriate to them in the teachings of theosophy there is conferred a title without external sign, an honour which brings, not the respect of other men, but inner peace. They feel the mystery weigh less heavily on them; they have discovered the possibility of creating their own hell or heaven; their scale of values for human things is more correct; they have acquired more compassion.

Just as Mme Blavatsky had not received the gift of physical beauty so she had no knowledge of the beauty of literary form; the surface of her philosophy is rough and uneven, while the body of her book is chaotic, shapeless, crushing, sexless like herself. It contains the doctrines of esoteric Buddhism, for what is called theosophy is the Buddhism of a school of Tibetan intellectuals. It is not Mme Blavatsky's own creation, nor did she ever claim that it was. She wrote without the help of any book and made frequent quotations from works only to be found in libraries to which she had no possibility of access. She wrote as a medium —all the evidence agrees on this point—at the dictation of Morya and Koot Houmi, and also of another Platonic initiate, who expressed himself only in French and belonged to a different group of initiates.

It is impossible to summarise, even shortly, the enormous mass of knowledge contained in *Isis Unveiled* and *The Secret Doctrine*. This knowledge comes from the ancient books preserved in Tibetan monasteries and goes back through civilisations to the very origin of man. This knowledge was so new and astounding to the arrogant thinkers of the West that they preferred to reject it *en bloc* without examination. Annie Besant, Steiner, Leadbeater* and others have nevertheless made every effort to clarify it and present it in a form accessible to the most ordinary intelligence. That has proved insufficient. Ordinary minds and great minds, both alike, have found that the light came from too great a distance, from a country which was not theirs, and that it was too dazzling. They need a lamp of a familiar kind, which lights up only the narrow circle of their inherited knowledge, their little prejudices, their commonplace ideals.

What a philosophy this is, which gives us the means of understanding the relationship of spirit and matter; of understanding how through the immemorial ages

* See Annie Besant's *Ancient Wisdom*, Steiner's *Outline of Occult Science*, and particularly M. Chevrier's *L'essai de doctrine occulte*, which is the clearest exposition of theosophical doctrines.

man has become individualised, has assumed successive bodies, to become more and more material on the descending curve of nature, and then to rise on the ascending curve; how he must accomplish the opposite task, that is to say, become spiritualised in order to be absorbed into the divine consciousness. This philosophy, which teaches us the law of reincarnation and the law of Karma, is the only system which lights up and to some small extent justifies what we see of a pitiless and incomprehensible universe. If we see—and it is possible for each one of us to do so if we try every day—that it is we who weave our own destiny, create the cause of our own happiness and suffering; if we know, beyond the possibility of a doubt, that every action taken against others is an action taken against ourselves—we come to the realisation that the world is perhaps not so unjust a place as it appears. And the moment we are aware that we live in a logical and ordered world, we understand that the only behaviour possible to us is obedience to that logic and that order; we are no longer troubled by injustice, for we regard ourselves as the sole cause of our own troubles. We seek a means for becoming happier by conforming to the current which carries us away. We bethink ourselves of preparing our future life if it is too late to obtain great results in this one. We realise that happiness as we see it is not the most important kind, and that there are scales of happiness parallel to our development. The search for a higher happiness leads us to see dimly that the source of the most ineffable joy lies in the spiritual development of our being. We learn the paths which lead there: meditation, silence of the soul and contemplation of that inner star which shines in our hearts, and the light of which, when we discover it in all its radiance, will make us one with the divine essence.

The bringing of the wisdom of the East might have been enough to arrest Western thought in its materialistic progress and to transform it. It did not do so. The dark shadow which follows every new thing spread over the woman who preached this doctrine of perfection. It was historically too late for the Inquisition to erect the martyr's stake for her. Nor was she stoned or crucified. But her contemporaries put her to the torture of doubt and contempt. The intellectuals either rejected her doctrine or persisted in ignoring it. It is true that it was not to them that her message was addressed. Theosophy, like all the great movements of the spirit, like Christianity and like the doctrine of the Albigenses, made its appeal to ordinary men, but it was misunderstood and unheeded by them. It is a strange example, of which we are the blind witnesses. The message came from far and from high. It is there, and yet to those who deny it it is useless.

As for the direct disciples of Mme Blavatsky, those who make use of her name, unconsciously or as a result of their own temperament, they have partly betrayed the meaning of the message in their explanation of it. There is a law which requires that every esoteric movement which is not, like the Albigensian movement, wrecked by total suppression should wither and petrify, be transformed into the hard stone of a Church, the icy marble of a dogma. Theosophy has become enveloped in the "religiosity" which its founder considered fatal. It began with the Christian adoration, the pious fervour, with which the Hindu masters were surrounded, though they certainly never asked it. The admonitions to an upright life were transformed into Anglican prudery. The sublime aims of brotherhood and of the development of spiritual powers were neglected in favour of expectation of the Messiah—the preoccupation of every sect in the world—which thenceforward occupied the first place. Buddhism, to which the founders of the theosophical movement had firmly attached themselves, was watered down and relegated to the background in favour of an esoteric Christianity. Finally, in order to satisfy men's need to pray in edifices, to see ritual altars, to be helped by the ceremonial magic of incense, candles and vestments, the theosophist leaders declared themselves bishops and, under the name of the Liberal Catholic Church, proceeded to build up that which Mme Blavatsky had laboured to destroy. They acted against the majestic message of theosophy, against the essential truth, against the law of the individual, of which Mme Blavatsky had been the inspired preacher.

Nevertheless this message, this truth and this law have not been lost. Mme Blavatsky's successors, in preparing their church, have brought up a young man, Krishnamurti, to be the head of it. But he, instead of proudly assuming the title of instructor of the world, which had been marked out for him, and of accepting an all-powerful papal mitre, has, with a greater pride, preferred to declare that he is "the possessor of the unconditioned and integral truth," and to wear the invisible mitre of the true sage. It matters little whether or not he has reached this sublime state. In any case he has returned to the teachings of Mme

Blavatsky and, paraphrasing certain texts of Sankara Acharya* and certain words of the Buddha, he has proclaimed them with the freedom that only youth can give.

He has repeated that all organisations and all Churches are barriers to understanding; that the new forms of worship and the new gods are no better than the old ones; that good intentions, good works or self-sacrifice are not enough if the inner veil of ignorance be not torn asunder; that all wisdom must be sought within oneself; and that it is by the development, the purification, the incorruptibility, of a man's inner "I" that he becomes one with the absolute.

* Sankara Acharya, who lived probably during the 9th century A.D., was a celebrated Indian theologian who wrote commentaries on the Bhagavadgita and the principal Upanishads.—*Trans.*

THE SADNESS OF THE MASTERS

AT Darjeeling, in Sikkim, on the borders of British India and Tibet, the mysterious door opens on the still unknown regions of the earth. Darjeeling is a fashionable hill town at the foot of the Himalayas where British society comes to recuperate after the burning climate of the plains. It is full of officials and tourists. But no one knows that the road which winds uphill and plunges into the deep mountain gorges is a road leading to another universe, a road as long and transcendent as Jacob's ladder.

It is by this road that explorers leave, in the interests of geography, or to bring back striking photographs, or because they are interested in ethnology. When these men of action come back they give lectures illustrated by lantern slides and tell us all about Lhasa, and the lamaseries perched on rocky heights like mediæval fortresses, and the colour of the Dalai Lama's robe. But actually they have seen nothing. They have seen nothing but a primitive population, stupid monks turning prayer wheels—nothing which attests the presence of the spirit.

How could they have perceived the presence of the spirit? With us, high culture is inseparable from material comfort and good manners, and is embodied in official institutions, universities or academies. It gives lectures, is preceded by a military band. In particular it is not concerned with moral development. How are they to believe that a man with a brown face—almost a nigger!—who forgets the body for thought, who sometimes remains motionless for days meditating in a cavern exposed to the snow; how can they believe that such a man may have views on science and philosophy which are more complete than those of the great European purveyors of ideas?

But men who cannot be seen by learned and intrepid explorers sometimes make themselves known to a man whose heart is filled with love.

It may happen that, in order to reach them and receive the word which is never written, a chosen Hindu or even a European goes to Darjeeling and starts out on the road which winds along the slopes of the Himalayas. This was done by Damodar, the comrade of the first theosophists, a Brahman who lost his caste to live with them. There came a moment when he felt that he was called. He was to go up among the high mountains. He had a bad cough and he was so thin that Mme Blavatsky said his legs were like sticks. He reached Darjeeling and started on his journey. He went in the direction of Lake Palti and the Kwen Lun Mountains, where once Mme Blavatsky had received her instruction. The head-porter of the caravan with which he travelled for some days stated that he had later found his clothes in the snow. He was never heard of again. It may be that, living on a little rice and the mountain air and sitting on the terrace of some lamasery, so high that no birds fly over it, he still tastes, scarcely aged by the passing of the years, the beatitude of the man who loves all things. Or perhaps he is long since dust at the bottom of some rocky gorge.

Mme Blavatsky said that in 1897 an occult door would be closed. No doubt the first step to this door was in Darjeeling, and she knew that about that time her instructors, having scattered the seed in the world, would be withdrawing their interest. The masters are no longer behind the theosophical movement. No longer does a letter arrive written on India paper without the intermediacy of the post, as happened to the first disciples. No longer does a grave face under a turban illumine a sleepless night. This form of the miraculous, which certain privileged persons undoubtedly experienced during several years, is no longer one of the possibilities of life.

In a pine-covered valley among the heights of the Kwen Lun Mountains two houses with roofs in Burmese style face one another across the valley. They are the houses of Morya and Koot Houmi. Between them, under the leaning trees, runs a narrow, clear stream spanned by an archaic bridge. Koot Houmi lives with his sister and has a Tibetan and his wife for friendly servants. Morya lives alone and rides on horseback every morning. They are now fifty years older than when their pupil Mme Blavatsky returned to the world, but the lifetime of a sage is at least three times as long as that of undeveloped man.*

When they meet near the little bridge over the stream and walk among the pines, they must sometimes remember

* The newspapers reported four or five years ago that a Russian explorer home from Tibet said he had spoken with a man " of a certain age " who had been Mme Blavatsky's instructor.

their past attempt to indicate the path to those who did not know it. Probably, for all their knowledge of men, they must still be surprised at their lack of success. If they do not feel bitterness when they remember that their names were derided and sensationalised by headlines in the newspapers, and became for many synonymous with mystification, they must yet admit to themselves that their effort was premature. Certainly they cannot despair of humanity, especially as they have attained a high degree of development and learned how to extend the limits of time. But if, by virtue of their gift of clairvoyance, they can see our cities and our machines, our passions and our selfishnesses, they must rejoice at their deep solitude and at the distance which separates them from us. They must tell themselves that they were highly unwise to reveal their existence some years ago to certain Englishmen, who, though perhaps well-intentioned, were decidedly limited in their outlook. Congratulating themselves on the folly which casts doubts on their existence, they must survey in contentment the height of the Himalayan peaks, the unchanging structure of the glaciers. They must think how fortunate it is for them that a mysterious power has seen fit to isolate Tibet from the so-called civilised world in order to allow Tibetans to cultivate the rare flower of intelligence. In the colossal dark cloud, which is for them the rest of the universe, they perceive, like flickering lights, like lamps just lighted, the minds of men awakening and calling to their elder brothers. How few and how dim are these lights! How slow are men to develop themselves! How many messengers will have to be sent out from century to century, messengers who themselves are imperfect and run the risk of falling back into the darkness! And perhaps, as they think of the length of time that must elapse, of the greatness of the efforts to be made, of the amount of evil in the world, the luminous eyes of the wise men grow dim.

EPILOGUE

THE history of these messengers is the history of a series of successive checks. They come, they exert an influence which is sometimes great, sometimes trivial, they meet with insult or death; and life resumes its course without any apparent trace of their passing.

What made the greatest impression on me, as I followed the story of their lives, was the fact that they were able to manifest themselves at all. It is surprising that the messengers were not suffocated when they were young, when the first light of the spirit shone out in their half-open eyes. Anger against that which is spiritual is so intense that even the fact of their manifestation must be regarded as amazing. It is amazing that Apollonius of Tyana should have died in extreme old age, and that Christian Rosenkreutz should have been able to shroud his person in a silence which no Dominican tribunal could break.

Disinterestedness, self-sacrifice, that which it is the convention to call *good*, do not, owing to their respect for life and their scruples of intelligence, possess means of defence or weapons equal to those of their enemies. Logically, evil and selfishness should always win, since they are bound by no restrictions. If, in spite of this, the essential conceptions which constitute the human ideal succeed in surviving, the reason is that there is in them a hidden force, a higher principle, which carries them on.

If you see a swimmer trying to fight his way to land through a rough sea, you think he will disappear every second. The forces that are combined to engulf him are tremendous. His head is often lost under the foam and we no longer see him. But the swimmer, through his skill and in virtue of the law which keeps a moving body on the surface, passes safely through the dangers and, contrary to all human expectation, gains the shore.

So it is with the courageous swimmers in the waters of life who are the bringers of the message. Ignorance spreads its shadow over them; hypocrisy beckons them downwards; pride blinds them. But a current of unknown origin, a submarine force of unknown attraction, drives them over the waves and allows them to attain their aim.

The message is brought regularly, in spite of the unceasing storm. It is always the same. It is contained in a few very simple truths, in a few words. It might be made into a written formula to mark the road. A man must be unselfish, despise money, become more and more intelligent, exercise his faculty of goodness. To this everyone replies: "I want to enjoy life and wealth, think only of myself, dominate others." The great battle of life is fought for no other prize than this. But the higher truths have to be presented to men in forms that are ever new. This is the duty which falls on the messengers, and the ungratefulness of the task is in direct proportion to the unconquerable selfishness of the human race.

The ideal is not the privilege of one race or of one particular place in the world. It has often been proclaimed by men who received it from no one, and, though they acted independently, their words were as sincere and as beautiful. Such was Ruysbroek, called the *doctor ecstaticus*, who rated the active life of the ordinary man as high as the life of the mystic in the sanctuary, and found the way to perfect union under the trees of ancient forests. Such was Giordano Bruno, who argued and discoursed in every city in Europe, and preferred the stake to the denial of his reason. Such was Swedenborg, who was interested in metallurgy and was also a hearty eater. Once, in a London hotel, he had a vision of a man bathed in light who told him that he, Swedenborg, had been chosen to interpret the Holy Scriptures and advised him to eat less heartily. Such was Jacob Boehme, the cattleman and apprentice to a Görlitz cobbler, who saw the flame of the divine love as he continued to hammer nails into soles.

Besides such men there have been others whose names are unknown because they cared little for fame, and truth radiated from them without their knowing it. There have been revealers who were unaware of the revelation that was in them; modest sages who mingled their wisdom with their daily life; timid magicians who did not know what magic was contained in a little act of kindness. We have all of us met, at least once in our lives, one of these unheralded initiators, and received from them a priceless gift, by a kindly word, a certain look of sadness, a sincere expression in the eyes.

For the message passes everywhere. Like hope and pain, it is essentially human. In order to hear it, it is not necessary to invoke at daybreak the Platonic intelligences, like Apollonius, or, like the ascetics, to practise mortification, or, like the Christian monks, to devote oneself to prayer. A man can understand it without knowing any philosophy, without belonging to any religion. It is accessible to the humblest, provided his mind and soul be open. Intelligence is not necessary; it is enough to desire intelligence. And the good intent to love is the sign that the message has been received.

THE END

INDEX